# Elections

*Written by Richard Rayburn*

*Illustrated by Cheryl Buhler, Theresa M. Wright, and Sue Fullam*

Teacher Created Materials, Inc.
P.O. Box 1040
Huntington Beach, CA 92647
©1992 Teacher Created Materials, Inc.
Made in U.S.A.

ISBN 1-55734-069-2

# Table of Contents

# Introduction

This is a book about elections and voting in the United States. It includes ideas, materials, and activities that can be used with students in the intermediate grades and middle school. The contents are divided as follows:

- First, information and practice activities to familiarize students with the terminology, practices, and traditions of American elections.

- Second, a game that challenges students to recall and apply what they learn.

- Third, a simulation activity to give students an opportunity to experience the election process first hand.

- Last is a teacher resource package that includes bulletin board patterns, research center ideas, a bibliography, and answer key.

Name: _____ Date: _____

# When Do You Vote?

Voting is more than a right guaranteed by the Constitution; it is an important part of everyday life in the United States. For example, how many times have you voted for something or someone?

Identify some of the things you have voted for in each of the following.

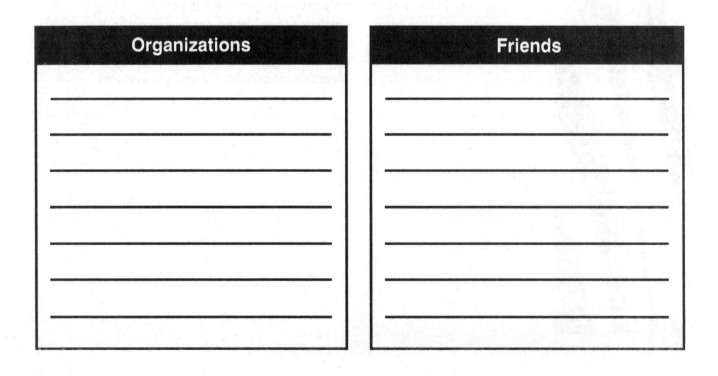

**Home**

**School**

**Organizations**

**Friends**

Name: _____     Date _____

# Voting at Home

Often times family members cannot agree about how to do something, where to go, what to do or when to do it. When this happens, sometimes family members make a decision by voting.

Describe a situation in which you and other members of your family made a decision by voting. Then answer the questions that follow.

**Situation:**

_____

_____

_____

_____

**What were the choices?**

_____

_____

_____

_____

**Who suggested voting?**

_____

_____

_____

_____

**How did the vote turn out?**

_____

_____

_____

_____

# Voting in an Organization

People who belong to organizations are often asked to vote about someone or something.  For example, teams select captains and clubs select officers and decide on rules, issues, or projects.

Recall a situation in which you were asked to vote as a member of an organization, such as a team, club, scout troop, church organization, etc.  Then answer the questions that follow.

**What was the issue or office?**

_____

_____

_____

_____

**What or who were the choices?**

_____

_____

_____

_____

_____

**How did you make up your mind how to vote?**

_____

_____

_____

_____

**What was the result?**

_____

_____

_____

_____

Name: _____    Date: _____

# Voting at School

During the school year there are usually many times you are asked to vote. One commonly held election is for school or class officers.

What elected officers do you have at your school? List them below.

**School**                                    **Class**

_____          _____

_____          _____

_____          _____

_____          _____

Draw a [☆] next to the offices that you would like to hold.

Place a [✔] next to the offices you have held before or hold now.

Place a [!] next to the offices that you are not allowed to hold.

What qualities do you think are necessary to win an election for a school office?

_____

_____

_____

What qualities do you think **should** be necessary to win an election for a school office?

_____

_____

_____

_____

# Basic Election Vocabulary

**absentee vote:** The vote cast by citizens who cannot go to their polling place on election day and therefore vote in advance or by mail using an absentee ballot.

**ballot:** A sheet of paper or a machine which presents a list of candidates and/or issues. It also indicates a voter's choices.

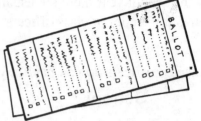

**candidate:** A qualified citizen who runs for political office.

**delegate:** A person who attends a convention as a representative of an area, such as a district or state. Delegates to one of the national political conventions vote to decide who the party's candidates for President and Vice President will be.

**Democratic party:** One of the two political parties in the United States having the greatest membership.

**district:** An area that is represented by a member of a legislative branch of government or other governing body.

**election:** A process of selecting one or more persons by voting. Elections held in the United States include general, primary, special, and runoff elections.

**election day:** The day when voters go to the polls to vote. The first Tuesday after the first Monday in November is election day for President and Vice President of the United States.

**elector:** 1. Anyone who is qualified to vote. 2. One of the 538 members of the electoral college.

**electoral college:** A group of 538 people (electors) who are chosen by the voters to officially elect the President and Vice President of the United States. They vote on the Monday after the second Wednesday in December.

**electoral vote:** The votes cast by electors in the electoral college for the President and Vice President of the United States. There are 538 electoral votes, with 270 needed to win. The candidate who gets the most popular votes in a state receives all of that state's electoral votes. The amount of electoral votes a state is worth is determined by combining the number of representatives and senators it has in Congress. For example, if a state has eight representatives and two senators, it is worth ten electoral votes. If Candidate A receives more votes than Candidate B in this state, no matter how close the vote, Candidate A gets all ten of the state's electoral votes.

**federal government:** The government for the entire United States of America.

**general election:** An election to choose among candidates for federal, state, and local office.

**majority:** In an election, more than half (fifty percent) of the total votes cast. For example, if 127 votes are cast, a majority is 64.

# Basic Election Vocabulary *(cont.)*

**national convention:** A gathering of Democratic, Republican, or other party delegates from each state. At the convention they choose their party's nominee for President and Vice President and vote on a party platform.

**nominee:** A person who is chosen to be a political party's candidate for an elective office.

**political campaign:** The contest for votes before an election among candidates for a public office.

**political party:** An organization of people who share similar ideas about how to govern the nation, state, and/or community. A political party attempts to gain power by electing its members to public office.

**poll:** 1.Counting votes in an election. 2. A place where people vote (polls or polling place). 3. A survey of people for their opinions.

**popular vote:** The actual number of votes cast for candidates for President and Vice President in a general election. The candidate who receives the most popular votes in a state wins all of its electoral votes.

**primary:** An election to choose a political party's candidates for office or other officials, such as delegates to a party's national convention. Primaries in the United States include closed, open, and blanket primaries.

**representative:** 1. A member of the House of Representatives; also called a congressman or congresswoman. 2. Any individual who makes decisions on behalf of others.

**Republican party:** One of two political parties in the United States having the greatest membership.

**vote:** Making a choice or decision in a formal way, such as by marking a ballot or raising your hand.

**voter:** A citizen who votes.

**voter registration:** The process before an election of signing up to vote, which includes identifying yourself and your place of residence.

# Extended Election Vocabulary

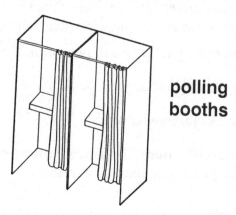

**barnstorming:** Making brief stops while touring rural or outlying areas during a political campaign.

**caucus:** A meeting of members of a political party. During caucuses, members select delegates to state or national nominating conventions. They also nominate state and local candidates. Several rounds of caucuses may be held. During the first round, voters gather in meeting places throughout a state.

**constituency:** The voters in a district that a legislator represents.

**incumbent:** The person who holds the office for which an election is being held.

**platform:** The basic principles, goals, and proposals of a political party.

**plurality:** The difference between the number of votes cast for the winning candidate and those cast for the candidate who comes in second. For example, if the winner gets 87 votes and the next closest candidate gets 63 votes, the winner's *plurality* is 24.

Also, when three or more candidates run for an office, the candidate who gets a plurality is the one who gets the most votes but whose total is not a majority. For example, if during an election 207 votes are cast, a majority is 104 or more. If the three candidates receive 74, 69, and 62 votes, no one has received a majority. Instead, the candidate with 74 votes has a *plurality*. Often times, this means that there will be a runoff election between the first and second place candidates.

**pollster:** An organization or individual that surveys people for their opinions.

**precinct:** A division of a city, town, or other local area. Usually a precinct contains about one thousand eligible voters.

**runoff election:** A second election held for an office when no candidate receives a majority of the votes in a general or special election. A runoff election is between the two candidates who polled the most votes in the first election.

**special election:** An election held to fill an office that has become vacant before the end of a term.

**suffrage:** The right, privilege, or act of voting.

BALLOT BOX

**polling booths**

# Elections and Voting
## What the Constitution Says

### Article 1

**Section 2.1.** The House of Representatives shall be composed of members chosen every second year by the people of the several States, and the electors in each State shall have the qualifications requisite for electors of the most numerous branch of the State legislature.

**Section 2.2.** No person shall be a representative who shall not have attained to the age of twenty-five years, and been seven years a citizen of the United States, and who shall not, when elected, be an inhabitant of that State in which he shall be chosen.

**Section 2.3.** Representatives shall be apportioned among the several States which may be included within this Union, according to their respective numbers.
The number of representatives shall not exceed one for every thirty thousand, but each State shall have at least one representative....

**Section 2.4.** When vacancies happen in the representation from any State, the executive authority thereof shall issue writs of election to fill such vacancies.

**Section 3.1.** The Senate of the United States shall be composed of two senators from each State, chosen...for six years...

**Section 3.3.** No person shall be a senator who shall not have attained to the age of thirty years, and been nine years a citizen of the United States, and who shall not, when elected, be an inhabitant of that State for which he shall be chosen.

**Section 4.1.** The times, places, and manner of holding elections for senators and representatives, shall be prescribed in each State by the legislature thereof; but Congress may at any time by law make or alter such regulations.

### Article II

**Section 1.1.** The executive power shall be vested in a President of the United States of America. He shall hold his office during the term of four years, and, together with the Vice President, chosen for the same term, be elected as follows:

**Section 1.2.** Each State shall appoint, in such a manner as the legislature thereof may direct, a number of electors, equal to the whole number of senators and representatives to which the State may be entitled in the Congress; but no senator or representative, or person holding an office of trust or profit under the United States, shall be appointed an elector. (See the Twelfth Amendment for more information about the election of the President and Vice-President.)

**Section 1.4.** The Congress may determine the time of choosing the electors, and the day on which they shall give their votes; which day shall be the same throughout the United States.

**Section 1.5.** No person except a natural born citizen...shall be eligible to the office of President; neither shall any person be eligible to that office who shall not have attained to the age of thirty-five years, and been fourteen years a resident within the United States.

# Elections and Voting (cont.)

## Amendment XII

The electors shall meet in their respective States, and vote by ballot for President and Vice President, one of whom, at least, shall not be an inhabitant of the same State with themselves; they shall name in their ballot the person voted for as President, and in distinct ballots, the person voted for as Vice President, and they shall make distinct lists of all persons voted for as President, and of all persons voted for as Vice President, and of the number of votes for each, which lists they shall sign and certify, and transmit sealed to the seat of the government of the United States, directed to the President of the Senate; the President of the Senate shall, in the presence of the Senate and House of Representatives, open all the certificates and the votes shall then be counted; the person having the greatest number of votes for President, shall be the President, if such number be a majority of the whole number of electors appointed; and if no person have such majority, then from the persons having the highest numbers not exceeding three on the list of those voted for as President, the House of Representatives shall choose immediately, by ballot, the President. But in choosing the President, the votes shall be taken by States, the representation from each State having one vote; a quorum for this purpose shall consist of a member or members from two thirds of the States, and a majority of all the States shall be necessary to a choice. And if the House of Representatives shall not choose a President whenever the right of choice shall devolve upon them, before the fourth day of March next following, then the Vice President shall act as President, as in the case of the death or other constitutional disability of the President. The person having the greatest number of votes as Vice President shall be the Vice President, if such number be a majority of the whole number of electors appointed, and if no person have a majority, then from the two highest numbers on the list, the Senate shall choose the Vice President; a quorum for a majority of the whole number shall be necessary to a choice. But no person constitutionally ineligible to the office of President shall be eligible to that of Vice President of the United States.

## Amendment XV

**Section 1.** The right of citizens of the United States to vote shall not be denied or abridged by the United States or by any State on account or race, color, or previous condition of servitude.

## Amendment XVII

The Senate of the United States shall be composed of two senators from each state, elected by the people thereof, for six years; and each senator shall have one vote. The electors in each State shall have the qualifications requisite for electors of the most numerous branch of the State Legislature.

When vacancies happen in the representation of any State in the Senate, the executive authority of such State shall issue writs of election to fill such vacancies: Provided, that the legislature of any State may empower the executive thereof to make temporary appointments until the people fill the vacancies by election as the legislature may direct.

# Elections and Voting (cont.)

### Amendment XIX

The right of citizens of the United States to vote shall not be denied or abridged by the United States or by any State on account of sex.

### Amendment XXII

No person shall be elected to the office of the President more than twice, and no person who has held the office of President, or acted as President, for more than two years of a term to which some other person was elected President shall be elected to the office of the President more than once.

### Amendment XXIII

The District constituting the seat of Government of the United States shall appoint in such manner as the Congress may direct:

A number of electors of President and Vice President equal to the whole number of Senators and Representatives in Congress to which the District would be entitled if it were a State, but in no event more than the least populous state; they shall be in addition to those appointed by the states, but shall be considered, for the purpose of the election of President and Vice President, to be electors appointed by a state; and they shall meet in the District and perform such duties as provided by the twelfth article of amendment.

### Amendment XXIV

The right of citizens of the United States to vote in any primary or other election for President or Vice President, for electors for President or Vice President, or for Senator or Representative in Congress, shall not be denied or abridged by the United States or any State by reason of failure to pay any poll tax or other tax.

### Amendment XXVI

The right of citizens of the United States, who are eighteen years of age or older, to vote shall not be denied or abridged by the United States or any state on account of age.

Name: _____     Date: _____

# Constitution Matching

Match the Article or Amendment with the best description. You may use each answer more than once.

a. Article I                    f. Amendment XIX

b. Article II                   g. Amendment XXII

c. Amendment XII                h. Amendment XXIII

d. Amendment XV                 i. Amendment XXIV

e. Amendment XVII               j. Amendment XXVI

_____ 1. Both men and women have the right to vote.

_____ 2. Electors shall vote for President and Vice President.

_____ 3. Eighteen year-olds may vote.

_____ 4. The District of Columbia is allowed three electoral votes.

_____ 5. Representatives must be at least 25 years old.

_____ 6. Citizens of all races have the right to vote.

_____ 7. Senators serve six year terms.

_____ 8. Senators are elected by the people of a state.

_____ 9. Representatives serve two year terms.

_____ 10. Citizens may not be charged a poll tax to vote.

_____ 11. The President serves a four year term.

_____ 12. The President may not serve more than two terms.

_____ 13. Senators must be a resident of the state they represent.

_____ 14. Each state shall have at least one representative.

_____ 15. The President must be at least 35 years old.

Name: _____     Date: _____

# Understanding the Articles of the Constitution

Use the Constitution to help you answer the following. Answer *yes* or *no* and explain your answer.

1. Mr. A was born in the United States. He has lived in the state of Maryland for twenty years. He is twenty-two years old, married, and the father of two children. Is he allowed to serve in the House of Representatives for his district in Maryland?

   _____Why? _____

   _____

   What part of the Constitution gives you this information?

   _____

2. Miss B is thirty-three and has been a citizen of the United States for six years. She has lived in the state of Alabama for one year. Is she allowed to serve as one of Alabama's senators?

   _____Why? _____

   _____

   What part of the Constitution gives you this information?

   _____

3. Mrs. C is a mother of four. She was born in France, but her parents are citizens of the United States. She has lived in foreign countries, but returned to live in the United States four years ago. She is fifty-five. Can she run for President?

   _____Why? _____

   _____

   What part of the Constitution gives you this information?

   _____

4. California has more citizens than any other state in the United States. Could the California state legislature pass a law giving it three senators in Congress because of its size?

   _____Why? _____

   _____

   Which part of the Constitution gives you this information?

   _____

5. Can the number of congressmen or congresswomen from a state be reduced?

   _____Why? _____

   _____

   Which part of the Constitution gives you this information?

   _____

# Understanding the Amendments to the Constitution

Identify the Amendment to the Constitution that helps you answer the following.

1. In 1856, citizens could be denied the right to vote because of their race.  Is this still legal today?

    _____Why? _____

    _____

2. In 1933, women could not be denied the right to vote.  Is this still true today?

    _____Why? _____

    _____

3. Franklin D. Roosevelt was elected President four times.  Would this be possible today?

    _____Why? _____

    _____

4. Do the people elect their senators?

    _____Why? _____

    _____

5. When you turn eighteen, will you be allowed to vote?

    _____Why? _____

    _____

6. Is it legal for the federal, state, or local governments to make you pay to vote?

    _____Why? _____

    _____

7. Before 1961, people living in the District of Columbia were not able to vote for electors for President of the United States.  Is this still true today?

    _____Why? _____

    _____

# Types of Elections

Use reference materials to discover the characteristics of each type of election listed below.

1. direct _____

   _____

2. indirect _____

   _____

3. nonpartisan _____

   _____

4. runoff _____

   _____

5. special _____

   _____

6. primary _____

   _____

7. closed primary _____

   _____

8. open primary _____

   _____

9. blanket primary _____

   _____

**Questions:**

10. Which type of election is used to choose the President and Vice President of the United States?

    _____

11. Which type of primary election does your state use?

    _____

# When Is Election Day?

Election day is the day when citizens go to the polls to vote. Each state picks its own election days for state and local elections. Election day for federal offices is the first Tuesday after the first Monday in November.

On each calendar mark an X on the Tuesday that would be a federal election day.

### November

| S | M | T | W | TH | F | S |
|---|---|---|---|----|---|---|
| 1 | 2 | 3 | 4 | 5 | 6 | 7 |
| 8 | 9 | 10 | 11 | 12 | 13 | 14 |
| 15 | 16 | 17 | 18 | 19 | 20 | 21 |
| 22 | 23 | 24 | 25 | 26 | 27 | 28 |
| 29 | 30 | | | | | |

### November

| S | M | T | W | TH | F | S |
|---|---|---|---|----|---|---|
| | 1 | 2 | 3 | 4 | 5 | 6 |
| 7 | 8 | 9 | 10 | 11 | 12 | 13 |
| 14 | 15 | 16 | 17 | 18 | 19 | 20 |
| 21 | 22 | 23 | 24 | 25 | 26 | 27 |
| 28 | 29 | 30 | | | | |

### November

| S | M | T | W | TH | F | S |
|---|---|---|---|----|---|---|
| | | 1 | 2 | 3 | 4 | 5 |
| 6 | 7 | 8 | 9 | 10 | 11 | 12 |
| 13 | 14 | 15 | 16 | 17 | 18 | 19 |
| 20 | 21 | 22 | 23 | 24 | 25 | 26 |
| 27 | 28 | 29 | 30 | | | |

### November

| S | M | T | W | TH | F | S |
|---|---|---|---|----|---|---|
| | | | 1 | 2 | 3 | 4 |
| 5 | 6 | 7 | 8 | 9 | 10 | 11 |
| 12 | 13 | 14 | 15 | 16 | 17 | 18 |
| 19 | 20 | 21 | 22 | 23 | 24 | 25 |
| 26 | 27 | 28 | 29 | 30 | | |

Find out when your state and community hold elections. Remember elections for governor, legislators, mayor, town or city council, school board, and special districts.

Name: _____     Date: _____

# Ballots

A ballot is a list of candidates and/or issues displayed on a printed form or a voting machine. Voters use ballots to indicate their choices in an election.

The names of different types of ballots are listed below. Find out what each ballot is and briefly describe it. Use the information you find to answer the questions.

1. Australian ballot _____

   _____

   _____

2. party column ballot _____

   _____

   _____

3. office-block ballot _____

   _____

   _____

4. short ballot _____

   _____

   _____

**Questions:**

5. Which type of ballot is used by all voters in the United States?

   _____

6. Do the voters in your state use a party column ballot or an office-block ballot?

   _____

**Bonus Question:**

   Where does the word **ballot** come from? _____

   _____

Name: _____          Date: _____

# Political Parties

A political party is an organization of people sharing similar ideas about how to govern the nation, a state, and/or a community.  There are several political parties in the United States today.  The two with the most members are the Republican party and the Democratic party.

Political parties try to get their members elected to federal, state, and local offices.  They raise money to pay for election compaigns and supply and organize workers to help their candidates.

Political parties have symbols that stand for them.  For example, the symbols of the Republican and Democratic parties are animals, the elephant and the donkey.

Make up a name for a political party. Write it here.

_____

Create a symbol for your party. Draw it in the box below. Add the name you created.

Name: _____          Date: _____

# Vocabulary Practice

*Fill in the blanks with election terms to complete the paragraphs.*

For the Larkins, today was an important day.  It was the first Tuesday after the first Monday in

November, _____ day.  Like many other citizens, they had gone to their polling place to
            **(1)**

_____.  On their _____ they put a mark next to the names of the _____
**(2)**            **(3)**                                          **(4)**

they wanted for each office.  Some of these were _____, people who already held
                                                **(5)**

the office and were running for re-election.  Others had just completed their first political

_____ for an office.  Most were members of the two largest political parties, the
      **(6)**

_____ and _____ parties.
         **(7)**                    **(8)**

Today's voting was part of a _____ election, because citizens were choosing
                              **(9)**

from among candidates for federal, state, and local offices.  As part of this, citizens were voting for the

_____ for President and Vice President of the United States.  In December these
       **(10)**

people would cast their votes as members of the _____college.
                                                 **(11)**

Mrs. Larkin has been especially interested in the presidential campaign because she was a

_____ to a national convention.  She had attended the convention because
        **(12)**

the person she supported for president had received the most votes in her state's _____
                                                                                   **(13)**

election.

Name: _____       Date: _____

# Check Your Election Vocabulary

*Fill in the blanks with the best word or words.*

1. A citizen who goes to the polls on election day and selects candidates on a ballot is

   a _____.

2. The two political parties with the largest membership in the United States are the

   _____ and _____ parties.

3. The first Tuesday after the first Monday in November is

   _____.

4. Voters mark their choices on a _____.

5. _____ represent their states at a national

   convention.

6. A person who runs for public office is a _____.

7. A political _____ is a contest for votes before an

   election.

8. The person with the most _____ votes becomes

   President of the United States.

9. If you cannot go to the polls on election day, you may cast an

   _____ ballot.

10. The candidate who already holds the office for which an election is being held is the

    _____.

Name: _____     Date: _____

# Our Elected Officials

Fill in the blanks with the information appropriate for where you live.

**Our Country: The United States of America**

    **President:** _____

    **Vice President:** _____

    **Senator:** _____

    **Senator:** _____

    **Representative:** _____

**Our State:** _____

    **Governor:** _____

    **Lt. Governor:** _____

    **Legislator:** _____

    **Legislator:** _____

**Our Community:** _____

    **Mayor:** _____

    **Council:** _____

    **Council:** _____

Name: _____     Date: _____

# How Often Do We Elect Our Officials?

Use reference books and other sources to find out how often elections are held for the offices listed below. Also identify the year in which the last election for each office was held and when the next will be.

1. President of the United States: _____

   Last election: _____ Next: _____

2. Senators: _____

   Last election for Senator #1: _____ Next: _____

   Last election for Senator #2: _____ Next: _____

3. Representatives: _____

   Last election: _____ Next: _____

4. Governor: _____

   Last election: _____ Next: _____

5. Legislators: _____

   Last election: _____ Next: _____

   Last election: _____ Next: _____

6. Council: _____

   Last elections: _____ Next: _____

7. Mayor: _____

   Last election: _____ Next: _____

**Name:** _____     **Date:** _____

# Local Elective Offices

Most states are divided into smaller areas called counties, parishes, or boroughs. There is another division called districts. Many of these areas are governed by elected officials.

Provide the information that applies to your area.

**County, Parish, Borough:**

(circle one)

Name: _____

Elective offices: _____

How often elected? _____

**Elementary School District:**

Name: _____

Elective offices: _____

How often elected?: _____

**High School/Secondary District:**

Name: _____

Elective offices: _____

How often elected?: _____

**Unified School District:**

Name: _____

Elective offices: _____

How often elected?: _____

**Community College District:**

Name: _____

Elective offices: _____

How often elected?: _____

Identify other special districts in which you live, such as water or transportation districts. Are these headed by elected officials? Write your findings on the back of this paper.

# State Legislative Bodies

Legislative bodies are groups of people who have been elected to make laws. The legislative body for the entire United States is called Congress. State legislative bodies are known by four different names. These names and the number of states that use them are listed below. Use this information to complete the graph.

General Assemblies          **19**          Legislative Assemblies          **2**

General Courts          **2**          Legislatures          **27**

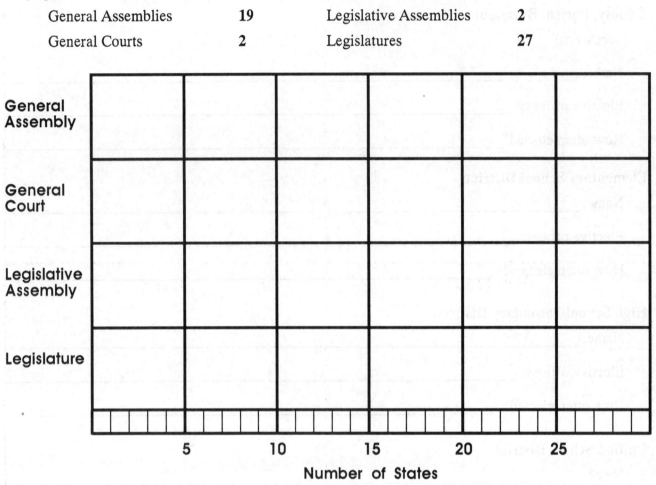

5. How many legislative bodies are there in all?

_____

6. What is the name of your state's legislative body?

_____

7. Circle the names of the houses in your state's legislative body. How often are there elections for the seats in each house? Write these numbers on the lines next to the names you circled.

_____Senate          _____House of Delegates

_____Assembly          _____General Assembly

_____House of Representatives

Name: _____     Date: _____

# Electing Representatives

In each box, write one election rule from the Constitution for a member of the House of Representatives.

| Age | Citizenship |
|---|---|
| | |
| **Residence** | **Term** |
| | |

1. The number of representatives a state has is based on its population.  What is the population of your state? _____

2. How many representatives does your state have? _____

3. About how many people does each representative represent? _____

4. If your state is large enough to have more than one representative it is divided into numbered areas, or congressional districts.  One representative represents each congressional district.   If your state is like this, what is the number of the district in which you live? _____

Name: _____       Date: _____

# Making Congressional Districts

All congressional districts must include about the same number of people.

Suppose the area below was a state with a population of three million, and you were asked to divide it into six districts.  How many people would you need to include in each district?_____

The numbers on the map stand for the number of people living in each rectangular area. Outline groups of connecting rectangles to create six equal sized districts.

| | | | |
|---|---|---|---|
| 50,000 | 100,000 | 50,000 | 50,000 |
| 10,000 | 100,000 | 500,000 | 100,000 |
| 100,000 | 500,000 | 50,000 | 100,000 |
| 50,000 | 90,000 | 10,000 | 50,000 |
| 100,000 | 500,000 | 50,000 | 100,000 |
| 50,000 | 50,000 | 90,000 | 150,000 |

Lightly color each district differently. Use the rectangles below to make a map key. To do this, color the rectangles to match the districts on the map.

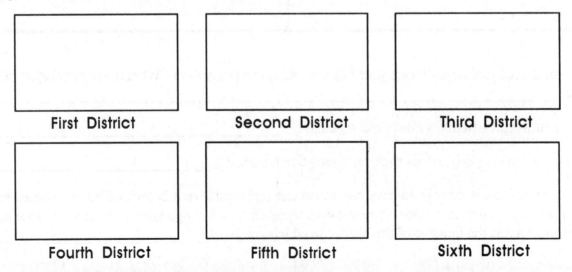

First District          Second District          Third District

Fourth District          Fifth District          Sixth District

# Electing Senators

In each box write one election rule from the Constitution for a United States senator.

| Age | Citizenship |
|-----|-------------|
| **Residence** | **Term** |

1. How many United States senators does your state have? _____

2. How many U.S. senators are there in all? _____

3. Unlike congressmen, senators do not all end their terms at the same time. Every two years, about one-third of the senate terms end. One year 34 senate terms end. How many end in each of the other two years? _____

4. A congressman represents one district in a state. How much of the state is represented by a senator? _____

5. The graph shows how the terms of senators are staggered. Add to the bars to show when the next election will be for each.

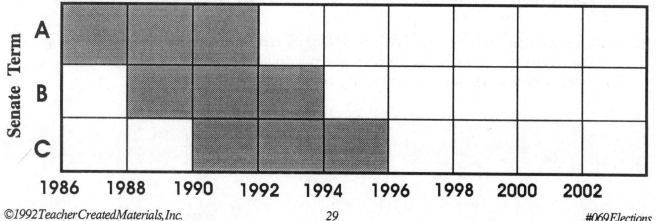

# Electing a President

Use this information to complete the "Electing a President" diagram on page 31.

1. Sometime before a presidential election year, political parties hold **State Conventions** in every state. Write State Conventions in the Party A and Party B boxes.

2. At most state conventions, delegates choose **Electors** for their party. The total number of electors chosen is 538. The number of electors the states choose is equal to the number of representatives and senators they have in Congress. Write electors in boxes E-A and E-B. Draw an arrow from Party A's State Convention to E-A and one from Party B's State Convention to E-B.

3. During the summer of a presidential election year, state delegates attend their parties' **National Conventions.** Write National Convention in boxes N-A and N-B.

4. At their national conventions, delegates choose a **Candidate** for president. Write Candidate in boxes C-A and C-B. Draw an arrow from N-A to C-A and from N-B to C-B.

5. On election day the **Voters** go to the polls. Write Voters in box V.

6. The **Voters** vote for the **Electors** who support their **Candidate**. Draw two arrows from the Voters box, one to each Electors box.

7. The group of Electors who receive the most votes in a state win the right to vote for the President. For instance, if in one state party A's electors get more votes than party B or party C, only party A's electors will meet to vote for President. Since electors have sworn to support their party, all of their electoral votes will go to their candidate. Draw an arrow from each Electors box to the appropriate Candidate box.

8. The Candidate who gets 270 or more electoral votes is declared the winner. Label box EV1 **270 +**. Draw an arrow from each candidate box to this EV1 box. From here draw one arrow to box US. Write **President of the United States** in this box.

9. If no candidate gets 270 or more electoral votes, the election goes to the House of Representatives. Write **Under 270** in box EV2. Draw a line from each Candidate box to EV2. Write **House of Representatives** in box HR. From EV2 draw an arrow to HR.

10. In a House election, each state gets one vote. (All of the representatives from a state vote. The candidate receiving the most votes gets the state's one vote.) The candidate who receives 51 or more votes is elected. Draw an arrow from the House box to the President box.

# Electing a President *(cont.)*

Use the information on page 30 to find out how the President of the United States is elected.

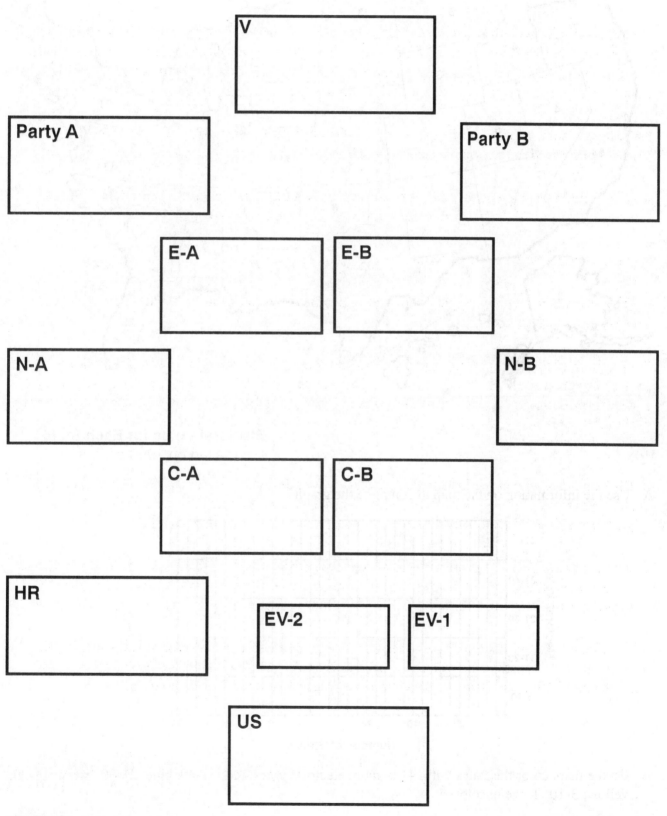

Name: _____     Date: _____

# Electoral Votes

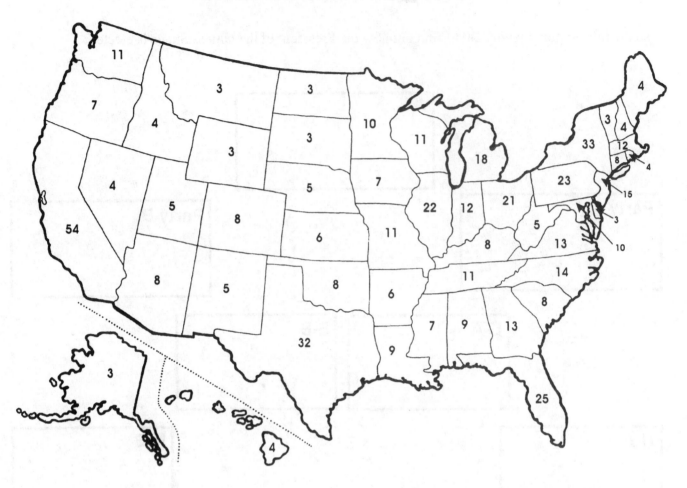

**Electoral Votes for Each State**
(based on 1990 census)

A. Use the information on the map to complete the graph.

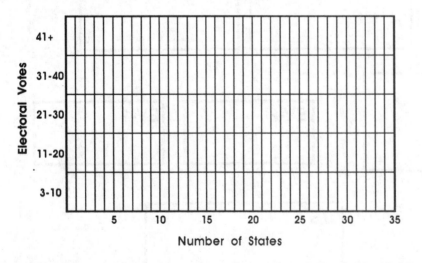

B. On the map, color the states with: 41 or more electoral votes, red; 31-40, blue; 21-30, green; 11-20, yellow; 3-10, leave uncolored.

Name: _____     Date: _____

# The Popular Vote

The actual number of votes cast for Presidential candidates on election day is called the popular vote. It is possible, though, that the candidate with the most popular votes may not become President. Do the following exercise to learn why.

This map shows five imaginary states and their value in electoral votes. Also shown are the popular votes cast in each state for Candidates A and B. Use this information to answer the questions.

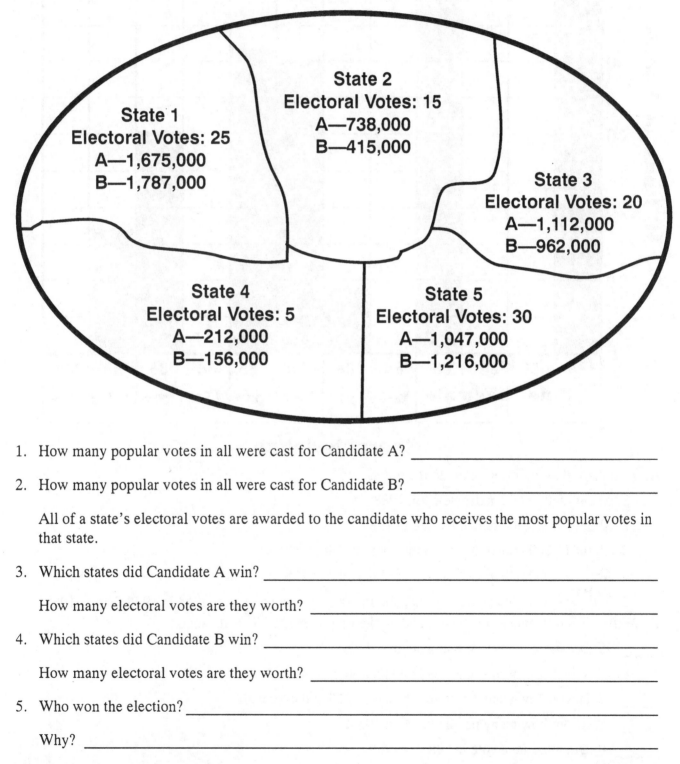

1. How many popular votes in all were cast for Candidate A? _____

2. How many popular votes in all were cast for Candidate B? _____

All of a state's electoral votes are awarded to the candidate who receives the most popular votes in that state.

3. Which states did Candidate A win? _____

   How many electoral votes are they worth? _____

4. Which states did Candidate B win? _____

   How many electoral votes are they worth? _____

5. Who won the election? _____

   Why? _____

Name: _____        Date: _____

# Compare the Popular Vote:
# 1984 and 1988

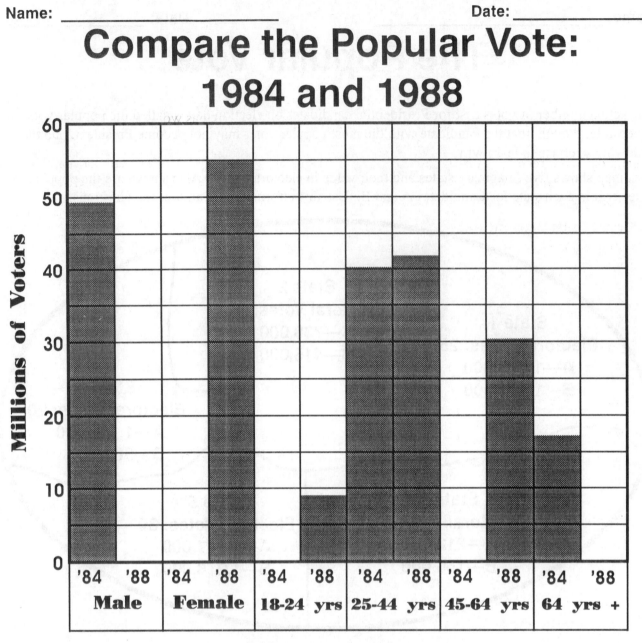

### Characteristics

A.  Add the following information to the graph.

    1. About 48,000,000 males voted in 1988.

    2. About 54,000,000 females voted in 1984.

    3. About 11,000,000 18-24 year olds voted in 1984.

    4. About 11,000,000 more 25-44 year olds voted in 1988 than did 45-64 year olds in 1984.

    5. In the 64 year old and over group, about 2,000,000 more people voted in 1988 than in 1984.

B.  Write YES if the answer can be found on the graph.  Write NO if it cannot.

_____  6. Did more women or men vote in 1988?

_____  7. Which group showed a decline in number of voters?

_____  8. How many women between the ages of 25 and 44 voted?

_____  9. About how many people voted in 1984?

_____ 10. Did more men vote in 1984 or 1982?

Name: _____     Date: _____

# Majority and Plurality

A candidate who receives more than one half (50%) of the **total** votes cast has won with a majority. For example, if a winning candidate receives 52% of the total votes, he has won with a majority of the votes.

A candidate who receives more votes than any other candidate but whose total is exactly half or less than one half of the **total** votes cast has a plurality. For example, if a winning candidate has 42% of the total votes cast in an election, he has won with a plurality of the vote.

Below are listed Presidents and the percentage of the popular vote they received. If they received a majority, write M on the blank. If they received a plurality, write P.

| | |
|---|---|
| ____ 1. John Quincy Adams - 31.9% | ____ 22. William Taft - 51.6% |
| ____ 2. Andrew Jackson - 56.0% | ____ 23. Woodrow Wilson - 41.9% |
| ____ 3. Andrew Jackson - 54.5% | ____ 24. Woodrow Wilson - 49.3% |
| ____ 4. Martin Van Buren - 50.9% | ____ 25. Warren Harding - 60.3% |
| ____ 5. James Polk - 49.6% | ____ 26. Calvin Coolidge - 54.0% |
| ____ 6. William Harrison - 53.0% | ____ 27. Herbert Hoover - 58.2% |
| ____ 7. Zachary Taylor - 47.3% | ____ 28. Franklin Roosevelt - 57.4% |
| ____ 8. Franklin Pierce - 53.6% | ____ 29. Franklin Roosevelt - 60.8% |
| ____ 9. James Buchanan - 58.1% | ____ 30. Franklin Roosevelt - 54.7% |
| ____ 10. Abraham Lincoln - 39.8% | ____ 31. Franklin Roosevelt - 53.4% |
| ____ 11. Abraham Lincoln - 55.2% | ____ 32. Harry Truman - 49.5% |
| ____ 12. Ulysses Grant - 52.7% | ____ 33. Dwight Eisenhower - 55.1% |
| ____ 13. Ulysses Grant - 55.6% | ____ 34. Dwight Eisenhower - 57.4% |
| ____ 14. Rutherford Hayes - 47.9% | ____ 35. John Kennedy - 49.7% |
| ____ 15. James Garfield - 48.3% | ____ 36. Lyndon Johnson - 61.1% |
| ____ 16. Grover Cleveland - 48.5% | ____ 37. Richard Nixon - 43.4% |
| ____ 17. Benjamin Harrison - 47.8% | ____ 38. Richard Nixon - 60.7% |
| ____ 18. Grover Cleveland - 48.5% | ____ 39. Jimmy Carter - 50.1% |
| ____ 19. William McKinley - 51.0% | ____ 40. Ronald Reagan - 50.7% |
| ____ 20. William McKinley - 51.7% | ____ 41. Ronald Reagan - 58.8% |
| ____ 21. Theodore Roosevelt - 56.4% | ____ 42. George Bush - 53.4% |

Which President received the largest majority? _____

Who received the smallest plurality? _____

# Republican Candidates

Below are listed the Republican Presidential and Vice Presidential candidates.  For each: 1. Mark an X in the box next to those elected President. 2. Circle the Vice Presidential candidates who later became President.  3. Fill in the blanks with the missing election years.

| | For President/Vice President | Year |
|---|---|---|
| ☐ | John C. Fremont/William L. Dayton | 1856 |
| ☐ | Abraham Lincoln/Hannibal Hamlin | 1860 |
| ☐ | Abraham Lincoln/Andrew Johnson | _____ |
| ☐ | Ulysses S. Grant/Schuyler Colfax | _____ |
| ☐ | Ulysses S. Grant/Henry Wilson | _____ |
| ☐ | Rutherford B. Hayes/William A. Wheeler | _____ |
| ☐ | James A. Garfield/Chester A. Arthur | _____ |
| ☐ | James G. Blaine/John A. Logan | _____ |
| ☐ | Benjamin Harrison/Levi P. Morton | _____ |
| ☐ | Benjamin Harrison/Whitelaw Reid | _____ |
| ☐ | William McKinley/Garret A. Hobart | _____ |
| ☐ | William McKinley/Theodore Roosevelt | _____ |
| ☐ | Theodore Roosevelt/Charles W. Fairbanks | _____ |
| ☐ | William Howard Taft/James S. Sherman | _____ |
| ☐ | William Howard Taft/James S. Sherman | _____ |
| ☐ | Charles Evans Hughes/Charles W. Fairbanks | _____ |
| ☐ | Warren G. Harding/Calvin Coolidge | _____ |
| ☐ | Calvin Coolidge/Charles G. Dawes | _____ |
| ☐ | Herbert Hoover/Charles Curtis | _____ |
| ☐ | Herbert Hoover/Charles Curtis | _____ |
| ☐ | Alfred M. Landon/Frank Knox | _____ |
| ☐ | Wendell L. Willkie/Charles L. McNary | _____ |
| ☐ | Thomas E. Dewey/John W. Bricker | _____ |
| ☐ | Thomas E. Dewey/Earl Warren | _____ |
| ☐ | Dwight D. Eisenhower/Richard M. Nixon | _____ |
| ☐ | Dwight D. Eisenhower/Richard M. Nixon | _____ |
| ☐ | Richard M. Nixon/Henry Cabot Lodge, Jr. | _____ |
| ☐ | Barry M. Goldwater/William E. Miller | _____ |
| ☐ | Richard M. Nixon/Spiro T. Agnew | _____ |
| ☐ | Richard M. Nixon/Spiro T. Agnew | _____ |
| ☐ | Gerald R. Ford/Robert J. Dole | _____ |
| ☐ | Ronald W. Reagan/George H. W. Bush | _____ |
| ☐ | Ronald W. Reagan/George H. W. Bush | _____ |
| ☐ | George H.W. Bush/Daniel Quayle | _____ |
| ☐ | _____  _____ | 1992 |

Name: _____     Date: _____

# Democratic Candidates

Below are listed the Democratic Presidential and Vice Presidential candidates.  For each: 1. Mark an X in the box next to those elected President. 2. Circle the Vice Presidential candidates who later became President. 3. Fill in the blanks with the missing election years.

| | For President /Vice President | Year |
|---|---|---|
| ☐ | Andrew Jackson/John Calhoun | 1828 |
| ☐ | Andrew Jackson/Martin Van Buren | 1832 |
| ☐ | Martin Van Buren/Richard M. Johnson | _____ |
| ☐ | Martin Van Buren/Richard M. Johnson | _____ |
| ☐ | James K. Polk/George M. Dallas | _____ |
| ☐ | Lewis Cass/William O. Butler | _____ |
| ☐ | Franklin Pierce/William R. D. King | _____ |
| ☐ | James Buchanan/John C. Breckinridge | _____ |
| ☐ | Stephen A. Douglas/Herschel V. Johnson | _____ |
| ☐ | George B. McClellan/George H. Pendleton | _____ |
| ☐ | Horatto Seymour/Francis P. Blair, Jr. | _____ |
| ☐ | Horace Greeley /B. Gratz Brown | _____ |
| ☐ | Samuel J. Tilden/Thomas A. Hendricks | _____ |
| ☐ | Winfield S. Hancock/William H. English | _____ |
| ☐ | Grover Cleveland/Thomas A. Hendricks | _____ |
| ☐ | Grover Cleveland/Thomas A. Hendricks | _____ |
| ☐ | Grover Cleveland/Adlai E. Stevenson | _____ |
| ☐ | William Jennings Bryan/Arthur Sewall | _____ |
| ☐ | William Jennings Bryan/Adlai E. Stevenson | _____ |
| ☐ | Alton B. Parker/Henry G. Davis | _____ |
| ☐ | William Jennings Bryan/John W. Kern | _____ |
| ☐ | Woodrow WilsonThomas R. Marshall | _____ |
| ☐ | Woodrow Wilson/Thomas R. Marshall | _____ |
| ☐ | James M. Cox/Franklin D. Roosevelt | _____ |
| ☐ | John W. Davis/Charles W. Bryan | _____ |
| ☐ | Alfred E. Smith/Joseph T. Robinson | _____ |
| ☐ | Franklin D. Roosevelt/John Nance Garner | _____ |
| ☐ | Franklin D. Roosevelt/John Nance Garner | _____ |
| ☐ | Franklin D. Roosevelt/Henry A. Wallace | _____ |
| ☐ | Franklin D. Roosevelt/Harry S. Truman | _____ |
| ☐ | Harry S. Truman/Alben W. Barkley | _____ |
| ☐ | Adlai E. Stevenson/John J. Sparkman | _____ |
| ☐ | Adlai E. Stevenson/Estes Kefauver | _____ |
| ☐ | John F. Kennedy/Lyndon B. Johnson | _____ |
| ☐ | Lyndon B. Johnson/Herbert H. Humphrey | _____ |
| ☐ | Herbert H. Humphrey/Edmund S. Muskie | _____ |
| ☐ | George S. McGovern/Sargent Shriver | _____ |
| ☐ | James E. Carter, Jr./Walter F. Mondale | _____ |
| ☐ | James E. Carter, Jr./Walter F. Mondale | _____ |
| ☐ | Walter F. Mondale/Geraldine A. Ferraro | _____ |
| ☐ | Michael Dukakis/Lloyd Bentsen | _____ |

# Other Political Parties—1

For most of the history of the United States, the President has been either a Democrat or a Republican. However, the nine men named below were neither Republicans nor Democrats. Using reference materials, find the name of the party of each of these Presidents.

1.  George Washington         _____

2.  John Adams                _____

3.  Thomas Jefferson          _____

4.  James Madison             _____

5.  John Quincy Adams         _____

6.  William Henry Harrison    _____

7.  John Tyler                _____

8.  Zachary Taylor            _____

9.  Millard Fillmore          _____

Using the grid, make a graph showing the names of the parties you found and the number of presidents that were members of each party.

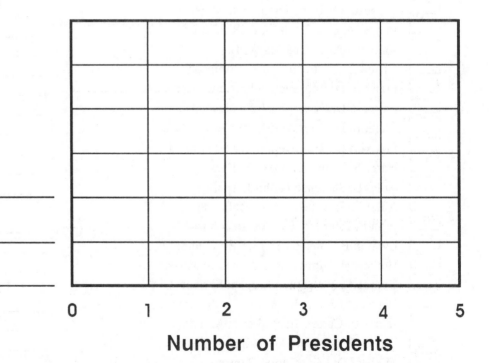

**Party Name**

**Number of Presidents**

Name: _____     Date: _____

# Other Political Parties—2

Usually in Presidential elections, several small political parties nominate candidates to run against the Republican and Democratic candidates.  Most of the time these smaller parties are not taken seriously. When a smaller party *does* attract a lot of attention, it is called a *third party*.  Third party candidates often attract millions of voters.  The most successful third party candidates for President and the years of their successes are listed below.

Use reference materials to discover the name of the third party to which each belonged and who the winning candidate was that year.

| *Candidate* | *Party* | *Winning Candidate* |
|---|---|---|
| 1. William Wirt (1832) | _____ | _____ |
| 2. Martin Van Buren (1848) | _____ | _____ |
| 3. Millard Fillmore (1856) | _____ | _____ |
| 4. John C. Breckinridge (1860) | _____ | _____ |
| 5. James B. Weaver (1892) | _____ | _____ |
| 6. Theodore Roosevelt (1912) | _____ | _____ |
| 7. Eugene V. Debs (1912) | _____ | _____ |
| 8. Robert M. LaFollette (1924) | _____ | _____ |
| 9. Strom Thurmond (1948) | _____ | _____ |
| 10. George Wallace (1968) | _____ | _____ |
| 11. John Anderson (1980) | _____ | _____ |

# Campaign Game

The Campaign Game gives students the opportunity to apply what they have learned about elections in the first part of this book. It is a board game for two to six players or teams. The object of the game is for each player/team (candidate) to accumulate votes as he/she moves along the "campaign trail."

To begin the game, participants decide how much of their campaigns will be dependent upon volunteer workers and how much upon money. As they move along the campaign trail, players encounter situations and problems (revealed on playing cards) which require the expenditure of man-hours, money, or staff expertise, and which will result in the addition or loss of votes.

Once all of the candidates have reached the end of the campaign trail, their votes are tabulated and the winner determined.

## Equipment

**Game Board:** The game board is divided into spaces which together make a trail on which players move their tokens. On the spaces are printed instructions to the players and the names of playing cards used during the course of play. It is recommended that the teacher copy, mount, and laminate the game layout sheet for small group use. For use with the entire class, copy the layout to a transparency and project it onto a screen.

**Playing Cards:** Three sets of 36 playing cards are provided. Eighteen of these cards have been left blank to allow teachers or students to add appropriate or current questions and situations.

- **Name the Term:** These cards require the students to identify election vocabulary terms, the names of public officials and offices, and other information related to elections and voting.
- **In the News:** These cards confront players with news items which often require them to choose between spending money and/or man-hours to gain or prevent the loss of votes.
- **Check the Polls:** These cards confront players with polling information that may help or hurt their campaigns, depending on how they respond to the situations.
- **Campaign Record Form:** These forms are used to record campaign resources, contributions, expenditures, and votes.
- **Tokens and Die:** These are supplied by teacher.

# Campaign Game

## Instructions

**Object of the Game:**

The teams/players move their tokens along the campaign trail by rolls of the die and, as they do so, attempt to collect as many votes as they can. The team having the most votes on election day is the winner.

**Preparation for Play:**

**Resource Distribution:** Each team/player begins play with 100 campaign resource points. Each point is worth $20,000 or 100 volunteer man-hours (one man-hour is an hour of work done by one worker). Teams/players must decide how many points to devote to money and how many to volunteer man-hours, with the total point value equalling 100. For example, a team/player that chooses to run a big money campaign might devote 90 of their 100 resource points to money ($1,800,000) and only 10 to volunteer workers (1,000 man-hours). An evenly balanced campaign would include a $1 million treasury (50 points) and 5,000 man-hours worth of volunteer labor (50 points).

**Campaign Record Form:** Teams/players record their expenditures and keep track of their votes on Campaign Record Forms. Before play begins, team/players record the distribution of their campaign resources on two forms, keeping one for themselves and giving one to the teacher or other designated master record-keeper. During the course of the game, expenditures in money and/or man-hours will be required to gain or protect votes, resources will be added to the campaign, and votes will be gained and lost. In all cases, the addition or subtraction of these numbers must be carefully recorded on Campaign Record Forms by teams/players and the designated master record-keeper.

**Rules of Play:**

1. To begin play, tokens are placed on the "Throw your hat in the ring" space. Teams/players move their tokens along the campaign trail by rolling the die and moving the number of spaces shown.

2. The instruction printed on the space on which the token lands is read, or a card is drawn from the deck named and it is read by a player from an opposing team.

3. After the question or instruction is read, the team/player provides an answer or decides what course of action to follow. The results of a correct answer or the decision are recorded on Campaign Record Forms.

4. Play proceeds until all team/player tokens reach Election Day. At this time vote totals are compared. The team/player with the most votes is the winner.

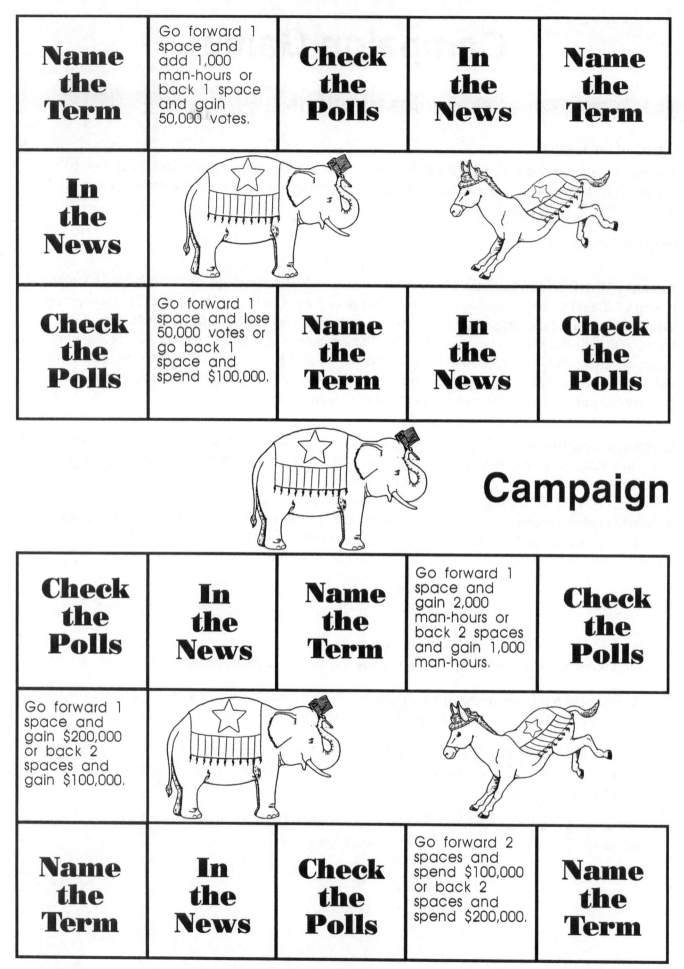

| Name the Term | Go forward 1 space and add 1,000 man-hours or back 1 space and gain 50,000 votes. | Check the Polls | In the News | Name the Term |
|---|---|---|---|---|
| In the News | | | | |
| Check the Polls | Go forward 1 space and lose 50,000 votes or go back 1 space and spend $100,000. | Name the Term | In the News | Check the Polls |

Campaign

| Check the Polls | In the News | Name the Term | Go forward 1 space and gain 2,000 man-hours or back 2 spaces and gain 1,000 man-hours. | Check the Polls |
|---|---|---|---|---|
| Go forward 1 space and gain $200,000 or back 2 spaces and gain $100,000. | | | | |
| Name the Term | In the News | Check the Polls | Go forward 2 spaces and spend $100,000 or back 2 spaces and spend $200,000. | Name the Term |

| Go forward 1 space and add 50,000 votes or back 1 space and add $100,000. | Check the Polls | In the News | Name the Term | START Throw your hat in the ring |

| Go forward 1 space and spend $100,000 or go back 1 space and lose 50,000 votes. | Name the Term | In the News | Check the Polls | Go forward 1 space and gain 100,000 votes or go back 2 spaces and gain 50,000 votes. |

Game

Name the Term

| In the News | Name the Term | Go forward 3 spaces and gain 100,000 votes or back 3 spaces and gain 50,000 votes. | Check the Polls | In the News |

| In the News | Check the Polls | Go forward 1 space and lose 100,000 votes or back 2 spaces and lose 50,000 votes. | Name the Term | END Election Day |

#069 Elections

| **Name the Term** | **Name the Term** | **Name the Term** |
|---|---|---|
| For 100,000 votes, name the place where people go to vote. <br><br> *poll or polling place.* | For 100,000 votes, name the President of the United States. | For 50,000 votes, name the major political parties in the United States. <br><br> *Democrat and Republican* |
| **Name the Term** <br> For 500,000 votes, name the amendment to the Constitution that gave black Americans the right to vote. <br><br> *fifteenth* | **Name the Term** <br> For 250,000 votes, name the Vice-President of the United States. | **Name the Term** <br> For 200,000 votes, identify election day. <br><br> *First Tuesday after the first Monday in November.* |
| **Name the Term** <br> For 100,000 votes, name the word used to describe someone who is running for office <br><br> *candidate* | **Name the Term** <br> For 500,000 votes, name the governor of our state. | **Name the Term** <br> For 500,000 votes, name the number of electoral votes our state has. |
| **Name the Term** <br> For 250,000 votes, name the type of election that is held to determine how many delegates a candidate will send to a national convention. <br><br> *primary* | **Name the Term** <br> For 500,000 votes, name the amendment to the Constitution that gave women the right to vote. <br><br> *nineteenth* | **Name the Term** <br> For 200,000 votes, name the term for a citizen who is qualified to vote. <br><br> *elector* |
| **Name the Term** <br> For 100,000 votes, name the title of the chief executive of a state. <br><br> *governor* | **Name the Term** <br> For 500,000 votes, name the amendment to the Constitution that lowered the voting age to eighteen. <br><br> *twenty-sixth* | **Name the Term** <br> For 100,000 votes, name a person who holds the office for which an election is being held. <br><br> *incumbent* |
| **Name the Term** <br> For 500,000 votes, name the political party of the current President of the United States. | **Name the Term** <br> For 100,000 votes, name the thing on which a voter indicates which candidates he or she is voting for. <br><br> *ballot* | **Name the Term** <br> For 500,000 votes, name the term for a contest for votes before an election for a public office. <br><br> *political campaign* |

| **Name the Term** | **Name the Term** | **Name the Term** |
|---|---|---|
| For 250,000 votes, name the term for voting in advance by people who cannot go to the polls on election day.<br><br>*absentee voting* | For 100,000 votes, name the document that lists the requirements for running for Congress and President.<br><br>*Constitution* | |
| **Name the Term** | **Name the Term** | **Name the Term** |
| For 50,000 votes, name the term for a survey of people for their opinion.<br><br>*poll* | For 250,000 votes, name the election that is held to choose between the two top vote-getters in a general or special election.<br><br>*runoff* | |
| **Name the Term** | **Name the Term** | **Name the Term** |
| For 50,000 votes, name the term for an organization that tries to get its members elected to public office.<br><br>*political party* | For 50,000 votes, name the process by which people are chosen for public office by voters.<br><br>*election* | |
| **Name the Term** | **Name the Term** | **Name the Term** |
| For 100,000 votes, name the body that officially elects the President and Vice President.<br><br>*electoral college* | For 250,000 votes, name a person who attends a national convention as a voting representative.<br><br>*delegate* | |
| **Name the Term** | **Name the Term** | **Name the Term** |
| For 50,000 votes, name the term for citizens who cast ballots during an election.<br><br>*voters* | For 100,000 votes, name the title of the chief executive of a city.<br><br>*mayor* | |
| **Name the Term** | **Name the Term** | **Name the Term** |
| For 100,000 votes, name the process by which citizens sign up to vote.<br><br>*voter registration* | For 500,000 votes, name the term for the basic principles, goals, and proposals of a political party.<br><br>*platform* | |

| In the News | In the News | In the News |
|---|---|---|
| Your candidate is photographed standing next to an organized crime figure. Lose 500,000 votes or spend 1,500 man-hours to repair the damage. | A newspaper reports that your candidate did not have to pay any state income tax last year. Donate $50,000 to the state or lose 100,000 votes. | A rich industrialist decides to support your candidate and helps raise money for your campaign. Add $100,000 to your treasury. |
| **In the News** | **In the News** | **In the News** |
| Your candidate's television commercial is ready. To show it statewide and pick up 200,000 votes, spend $500,000. To show it in a smaller area for 100,000 votes, spend $300,000. | During a television appearance, the interviewer asks all the questions that the staff practiced with your candidate. Add 100,000 votes. | Your candidate and 100 volunteers join in a 10K race for charity. Gain 50,000 votes for 200 man-hours and $10,000. |
| **In the News** | **In the News** | **In the News** |
| The President can't remember your candidate's name during a news conference. Spend $100,000 for extra advertising or lose 50,000 votes. | A famous movie star endorses your candidate on a popular talk show. Add 50,000 votes at a cost of $10,000 to pay for the use of the star's name in your ads. | Your candidate's brother uses campaign workers and money to remodel his house. Lose 0 votes, but pay $50,000 and 500 man-hours. |
| **In the News** | **In the News** | **In the News** |
| Your candidate's spouse is reported to be under investigation for misuse of campaign funds. Lose 250,000 votes or spend $200,000 and 1,000 man-hours to repair the damage. | A rock star popular with young teenagers endorses your candidate during a concert. Pay $10,000 to avoid losing 50,000 votes. | Three famous astronauts appear with your candidate at a rally. Add 50,000 votes at a cost of $50,000. |
| **In the News** | **In the News** | **In the News** |
| Your candidate is shown on the network news helping pick up trash on a public beach. Add 50,000 votes at a cost of 500 man-hours. | Your candidate kisses babies for the cameras and starts a flu epidemic. Lose 500,000 votes unless you spend $200,000 and 1,000 man-hours. | A famous author releases an unauthorized biography of your candidate. Lose 100,000 votes unless you spend $200,000 to buy up all the copies. |
| **In the News** | **In the News** | **In the News** |
| You send 500 of your candidate's supporters to help with disaster relief at a flood site. Pick up 200,000 votes at a cost of 2,000 man-hours. | Your candidate makes a hole-in-one during a celebrity golf tournament. Add 50,000 votes but pay $5,000 to the golf pro who gave the lessons. | You want to buy space for a full-page ad in three important newspapers. Gain 100,000 votes if you spend the $50,000. |

| In the News | In the News | In the News |
|---|---|---|
| Your candidate helps catch a mugger during a campaign stop. Gain 500,000 votes. | Your media consultant buys commercial time during professional wrestling shows. Gain 0 votes at a cost of $250,000 for commercial time and $50,000 for a new consultant. | |
| A newspaper tabloid claims that your candidate once saw Bigfoot. Gain 50,000 votes. | Your candidate shows up for a fundraiser on the wrong day. Gain no votes at a cost of 500 man-hours. | |
| Your candidate is voted one of the 10 best dressed Americans. Gain 50,000 votes. | Your candidate comes out in favor of a redevelopment plan. Gain $50,000 in donations from developers but lose 100,000 votes from homeowners. | |
| Your candidate and 100 workers join in a neighborhood cleanup project. Gain 100,000 votes at a cost of 500 man-hours. | A giant rally for your candidate draws a huge crowd. Gain 250,000 votes for $100,000 and 2,000 man-hours. | |
| Your candidate comes down with pneumonia. Spend $100,000 and 1,000 man-hours or lose 100,000 votes. | Your candidate spends a day with a poor family. Gain 100,000 votes for 100 man-hours. | |
| The postage rate goes up $.03. Set aside $30,000 for the extra cost or lose 100,000 votes. | The newspapers bury a story about your candidate's successful rally. Gain 50,000 votes for $100,000 and 2,000 man-hours. | |

| **Check the Polls** | **Check the Polls** | **Check the Polls** |
|---|---|---|
| Younger voters think your candidate is too old. Spend $100,000 to change this impression or lose 50,000 votes. | Polls show that your candidate's opponents are gaining ground. Spend $100,000 and 1,000 man-hours or give each of the other players 100,000 votes. | Polls show that your candidate is luring voters away from opponents. Take 50,000 votes away from each of the other players. |
| **Check the Polls** | **Check the Polls** | **Check the Polls** |
| Senior citizens think your candidate is too young. Spend $100,000 to change this impression or lose 50,000 votes. | Your candidate is perceived to be sensitive about environmental issues. Add $100,000 to your treasury and 100,000 votes. | Voters don't think your candidate is religious enough. Lose 100,000 votes. |
| **Check the Polls** | **Check the Polls** | **Check the Polls** |
| Spend $100,000 to conduct your own poll. Pick up 50,000 votes by using what you learn from the results. | No one seems to understand your candidate's stand on gun control. Spend $200,000 and 1,000 man-hours to clarify it. | Voters think your candidate is too religious for the area. Lose 100,000 votes. |
| **Check the Polls** | **Check the Polls** | **Check the Polls** |
| Your candidate's standing in all polls is slipping. Spend 1,000 man-hours and $100,000 or lose 50,000 votes. | A poll of middle-income voters indicates that they believe you support their interests. Gain 250,000 votes, $100,000, and 2,000 man-hours. | Your support in minority neighborhoods is slipping. Spend $100,000 and 1,000 man-hours to improve your image or lose 100,000 votes. |
| **Check the Polls** | **Check the Polls** | **Check the Polls** |
| Minority groups strongly support your candidate. Add $100,000 and 1,000 man-hours to your campaign. | A poll of wealthier voters indicates that they believe you support their interest. Lose 200,000 votes and 2,000 man-hours but gain $250,000. | High school students think your candidate is the best. Gain 0 votes but add 1,000 man-hours. |
| **Check the Polls** | **Check the Polls** | **Check the Polls** |
| Poll shows that voters prefer candidates who drive expensive cars. Spend $100,000 for a luxury car or lose 50,000 votes. | The presidential candidate for your party is taking a beating in the polls. Lose 100,000 votes unless you spend $100,000 on damage control. | A poll of middle-aged voters shows that your candidate is perceived as soft on crime. Spend $250,000 and 2,000 man-hours or lose 500,000 votes. |

| Check the Polls | Check the Polls | Check the Polls |
|---|---|---|
| Polls show that your candidate is not trusted by voters under thirty. Spend $500,000 and 1,000 man-hours to change their minds or lose 250,000 votes. | Voters think you are running a dirty campaign. Give 50,000 votes to each opponent and dismiss 50 staffers at a cost of 4,000 man-hours. | |
| **Check the Polls** | **Check the Polls** | **Check the Polls** |
| A poll of urban voters shows that your candidate is popular with them. Each opponent must spend $250,000 and 4,000 man-hours to try to win them back or give you 200,000 votes. | Polls show that voters like tall candidates. Your candidate is 6 feet 3 inches tall. Gain 100,000 votes. | |
| **Check the Polls** | **Check the Polls** | **Check the Polls** |
| A poll of rural voters shows that your candidate is popular with them. Each opponent must spend 2,000 man-hours and $50,000 to win them back or give you 50,000 votes. | Polls show that voters want taxes cut, but your candidate doesn't agree. Give 100,000 votes to each opponent who spends $250,000 to exploit this issue. | |
| **Check the Polls** | **Check the Polls** | **Check the Polls** |
| In a poll of psychics your candidate is picked to win the election. Take 50,000 votes from each opponent who does not pay $50,000 for their own poll. | Polls show that voters think your candidate has the best leadership qualities. Take 100,000 votes from each opponent. | |
| **Check the Polls** | **Check the Polls** | **Check the Polls** |
| A poll of suburban voters shows that your candidate is popular with them. Each opponent must spend 3,000 man-hours and $200,000 or give you 100,000 votes. | A poll shows that your candidate is popular with most female voters. Take 100,000 votes from each opponent who does not give up $250,000 and 2,000 man-hours. | |
| **Check the Polls** | **Check the Polls** | **Check the Polls** |
| A poll shows that voters think your candidate is weak on economics. Give each opponent 50,000 votes unless you spend $100,000 and 1,000 man-hours to change this perception. | Polls show that your candidate is disliked by most male voters. Give up 100,000 votes to each opponent unless you spend $250,000 and 2,000 man-hours. | |

# Campaign Record Form

## Campaign Resources:

Beginning total = 100 points

1 point = $20,000 or 100 man-hours

| Money in campaign treasury at start of play: | Volunteer man-hours at start of play: | Votes at start of play: |
|---|---|---|
| _____ points = $ _____ | _____ points = _____ hrs. | 500,000 |
| debt/credit _____ <br> new total = _____ | debt/credit _____ <br> new total = _____ | (+/-) _____ <br> = _____ |
| debt/credit _____ <br> new total = _____ | debt/credit _____ <br> new total = _____ | (+/-) _____ <br> = _____ |
| debt/credit _____ <br> new total = _____ | debt/credit _____ <br> new total = _____ | (+/-) _____ <br> = _____ |
| debt/credit _____ <br> new total = _____ | debt/credit _____ <br> new total = _____ | (+/-) _____ <br> = _____ |
| debt/credit _____ <br> new total = _____ | debt/credit _____ <br> new total = _____ | (+/-) _____ <br> = _____ |
| debt/credit _____ <br> new total = _____ | debt/credit _____ <br> new total = _____ | (+/-) _____ <br> = _____ |
| debt/credit _____ <br> new total = _____ | debt/credit _____ <br> new total = _____ | (+/-) _____ <br> = _____ |
| debt/credit _____ <br> new total = _____ | debt/credit _____ <br> new total = _____ | (+/-) _____ <br> = _____ |
| debt/credit _____ <br> new total = _____ | debt/credit _____ <br> new total = _____ | (+/-) _____ <br> = _____ |
| debt/credit _____ <br> new total = _____ | debt/credit _____ <br> new total = _____ | (+/-) _____ <br> = _____ |
| debt/credit _____ <br> new total = _____ | debt/credit _____ <br> new total = _____ | (+/-) _____ <br> = _____ |
| debt/credit _____ <br> new total = _____ | debt/credit _____ <br> new total = _____ | (+/-) _____ <br> = _____ |
| debt/credit _____ <br> new total = _____ | debt/credit _____ <br> new total = _____ | (+/-) _____ <br> = _____ |

# Simulation

The following pages include guidelines, ideas, and materials for conducting an election campaign. The complexity and duration of this activity is dictated by the number of ideas and/or materials the teacher wishes to employ and amount of the student body to involve. The simulation involves declarations of candidacy and the creation of parties, campaign staffs, and an Election Board to oversee the campaign. These elements are combined to conduct a mock election. Possible features to include in the simulation are campaign money and expenses, surveys, voter registration, and various advertising media.

# Getting Started

Before you do anything else, you may want to consider the following.

## What will the election be for?

There are three basic kinds of elections you can consider:

- One in which votes are cast for candidates.
- One in which votes are cast for or against a proposal.
- One which combines both 1 and 2.

If you wish to conduct an election which pits candidates against each other, you may wish to use the simulation as a tool for selecting student body, class, or grade level officers. Or, you may wish to have the students choose from actual national, state, or local candidates. Be sure students have accurate information about the candidates and their positions on important issues. A third way is to create fictitious candidates for whom you assign positions on issues created expressly for your simulation.

If you choose to have the students vote on a proposal, consider confronting them with a school, local, state, or national issue or create a hypothetical one.

## Who do you involve?

Involve as much of the student body in your electorate as possible. If involving the entire student body is not practical or desirable, try using several grades, or at the least, your grade level.

## How elaborate do you want the simulation to be?

Examine the following pages and choose those elements that appeal to you or are the most practical. The more features you include, the more realistic and rewarding the simulation will be.

52

# Organizing Campaign Staffs

Assign students to candidates or proposals, or have them choose for themselves. Once the members of each group have been identified, arrange or have them arrange themselves into campaign staffs. Each staff should record the identity of their candidate/position and staffers, such as campaign manager, treasurer, press secretary, speech writers, pollsters, data processors, and other campaign workers (see page 61). This document should be submitted to the teacher and/or election board.

## Suggested Staffers

**campaign manager:** This person is in charge of and manages the campaign staff. He or she sees that other members of the staff know their duties and carry them out prompty and effectively. He or she consults with other members of the staff to determine campaign strategy.

**treasurer:** This person is necessary if you employ campaign "money" in your simulation. He or she is responsible for holding, disbursing, and keeping track of the campaign's funds.

**press secretary:** This person is responsible for notifying the electorate of events that the campaign is planning and for overseeing the production and placement of advertisements in the school newspaper, flyers, posters, banners, and other campaign paraphernalia.

**speech writers:** Two or more people who, at the direction and with the help of the candidate and campaign manager, write speeches for the candidate and his/ her supporters and who create scripts for audio and/or video advertisements.

**pollsters:** Two or more people who conduct polls on behalf of the campaign to determine the positions of the voters. They submit their surveys to the data processors.

**data processors:** Two or more people to whom surveys are submitted and who record the information and compile it in such a way as to be easily understood by the rest of the staff. They may also work with the treasurer to keep track of the budget.

**campaign workers:** These are staffers who help in any way possible.

## Choosing an Official Symbol

Allow students from each campaign to meet and design an official symbol for use by their party. The symbol can appear in campaign literature and in commercials. (See page 62)

# The Election Board

The election board is composed of students who are not connected with any campaign and who work with the teacher to oversee the conduct of the simulation. It is recommended that an election board be formed if most or all of the simulation features are employed and especially when campaign "money" is used.

The duties that the election board might perform are listed below. Select those appropriate for your class. Indicate this by putting a check in the box next to the duty. Have students sign up for those duties you have checked off.

## Election Board Duties

| Necessary Duties | Job Description | Student Sign-Up |
|---|---|---|
| ☐ | Issuing funds to campaign treasurers. | _____ |
| ☐ | Receiving "payments" from campaign treasurers for campaign expenses. | _____ |
| ☐ | Examination and approval of all campaign literature and other forms of advertisement. | _____ |
| ☐ | Distribution and reception of voter registration forms and responsibility for recording, printing, and distributing lists of registered voters. | _____ |
| ☐ | Recording and filing all campaign documents, including staff lists and party names and symbols. | _____ |
| ☐ | Printing and distributing ballots. | _____ |
| ☐ | Manning and monitoring polling places. | _____ |
| ☐ | Collecting and counting ballots. | _____ |
| ☐ | Investigating and ruling on disputes and challenges. | _____ |
| ☐ | Declaring the winner of the election. | _____ |

# Registering Voters

**Procedure:**

Using the voter registration cards (page 63) or those of your own design, have members of the Election Board and/or campaign staffs register the simulation population. Establish a suitable period of time during which students will be allowed to register.

**Preparation:**

Duplicate and distribute voter registration cards (page 63) to the Election Board and/or campaign staffs.

Provide card tables, desks, etc., at which students can register voters at suitable times on the playground, in the hallway, or in other accessible locations.

Make sure that students file the registration cards carefully by some prearranged method, such as alphabetically by class.

## Sample Record Sheet

**Registered Voters—Room** _____  **Grade** _____  **Number of Students:** _____

| Name: | Date Registered: | Party: |
|---|---|---|
| 1 | | |
| 2 | | |
| 3 | | |
| 4 | | |
| 5 | | |
| 6 | | |
| 7 | | |
| 8 | | |
| 9 | | |
| 10 | | |
| 11 | | |
| 12 | | |
| 13 | | |
| 14 | | |
| 15 | | |
| 16 | | |
| 17 | | |
| 18 | | |
| 19 | | |
| 20 | | |
| 21 | | |
| 22 | | |

# Conducting a Poll

An election survey form (page 64) is provided for use during the simulation or as a model for the development of your own form.

While there are three sections on the form provided, pollsters need not use all three at once. In fact, a campaign staff may prefer to use each section as an individual poll.

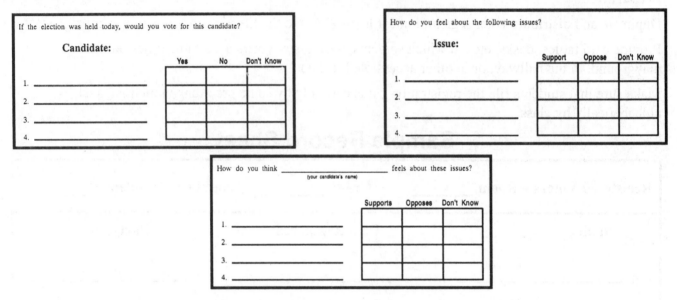

It is suggested that the students follow five steps when setting to work to conduct a poll.

1. **Set a Goal:** Decide what you want to find out from your survey. For example, does the campaign want to know how much of the electorate favors their candidate at any one time, or is it more important to know what issue(s) is the most important or interesting to the electorate?

2. **Select a Sample:** Decide who you want to question. For example, do you want to survey all the electorate or a cross-section, one grade level, only girls or boys, or students at random?

3. **Design a Questionnaire:** Will you use the form provided, find an example from elsewhere, or make up your own?

4. **Collect the Information:** There are two possible methods for collecting the information you want at school. One way is to interview the individuals you want to survey and mark their responses on the form. The other method is to distribute questionnaires and have individuals fill them out on their own.

5. **Tabulate and Analyze:** After the surveys have been returned, record the responses on a computer or a tally sheet. Organize the information on a chart, such as a graph or table, so that it is easy to read. Discuss the information and decide how to make use of it.

# Primaries, Conventions, and Electoral Votes

If you are to simulate a Presidential election, consider incorporating primaries, conventions, and/or electoral votes in your simulation.

**Primaries:** These are particularly useful if you have several students or fictitious candidates in the running and a narrower field is preferred.

Begin by assigning candidates to one of two parties. After voters have been registered and brief primary campaigns have been conducted, have the electorate vote in a closed primary format. If this is too complicated, simply hold an open primary in which all but the two top candidates are eliminated. The runoff election then becomes the basis for the rest of the simulation.

**Conventions:** After voters have been registered, have them meet in separate party conventions to choose their candidate. In these conventions, students should sit in classroom groups to simulate state delegations. Speeches by the candidates are followed by voting in each delegation. After voting, the chairman of each delegation announces the the results of their vote during a roll-call of classes.

An alternative to this would be a convention of the entire electorate. Meeting as classroom delegations, the students would vote to reduce a crowded field to two candidates.

**Electoral Votes:** To simulate a presidential election, give the participating classes a point value. The value of the classes could be the same, or they could be varied according to class size, age of students, etc. As in a presidential election, the candidate receiving the most votes in a class would receive all of its points (electoral votes). The candidate with the most **points** would then be the winner. Some form of tie-breaking process should be established before the election if this idea is used. For example, you might leave it to the student council to decide the winner.

# The Polling Place

1. The illustration and list on this page suggest a plan for a polling place for your simulation. Your polling place will need:

   - polling booths
   - ballots
   - receipts for ballots. *(This can be a tear-off.)*
   - ballot box
   - U.S. flag

   - table and chairs
   - chart with voting directions
   - registered voters lists
   - pens or pencils
   - state flag

2. Ideally, polling booths should be large enough for the students to enter. Since schools are often used as polling places, it might be possible to borrow actual polling booths that are being stored on campus. If not, try obtaining some refrigerator boxes from a local appliance store and adding a curtain. Less dramatic, but just as effective are table-top booths.

3. Encourage election board members to dress appropriately.

4. Whatever the style, it is strongly recommended that voting occur at one or more polling places, rather than simply distributing ballots in classrooms, so that the flavor of a real election is maintained.

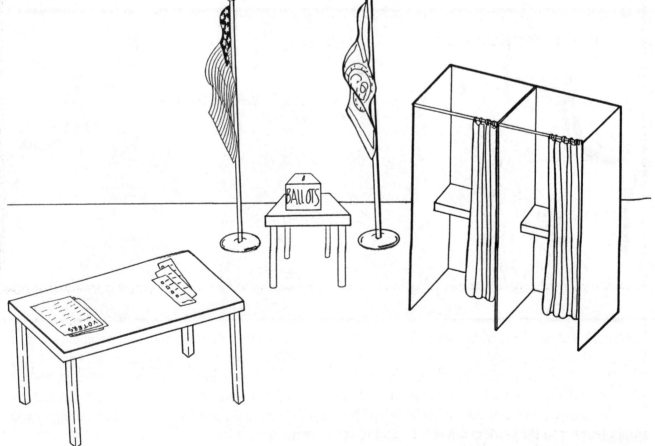

# Campaign Expenses

To simulate the financial cost of an election campaign, have students use play campaign money (page 65) to pay for "expenses."

Distribute campaign money to the treasurers of the parties. The amount suggested for each candidate is $1,115,000 (five $100,000's; ten $50,000's; ten $10,000's; fifteen $1,000's; or the equivalent of five campaign money sheets).

The candidate and his/her staff must decide how they will budget their money to cover their expenses. These expenses might include:

| | |
|---|---|
| **television advertising** | $1,000,000 to present a video-taped message to each classroom |
| **radio advertising** | $500,000 to present an audio only message to each classroom |
| **conducting a rally** | $500,000 |
| **posters** | $10,000 per poster per week |
| **fliers** | $1,000 per printing |
| **mailers** | $1,000 per mailing |

The Election Board might be given responsibility for distributing and collecting campaign money and overseeing its use.

# Producing a Campaign Commercial

Producing a commercial for your campaign may be just the thing you need to reach the electorate with your message. Make a radio (audio tape) or television (video tape) message and circulate it through the other classrooms.

If school recording equipment is not available for your use or it is not convenient to tape messages at school, perhaps a parent would be willing to help you produce your message.

**What you will need:**

1. Recording equipment; either a cassette recorder with a microphone or a video camera, preferably with a remote microphone.

2. A quiet place to record your message. If you intend to make a video recording, choose a simple, well lit, attractive background, such as a bookcase, curtains, or a fireplace.

3. A script. This is the single most important element. Make your message brief, to the point, and easy to read. Include what you think are the one or two most important things you think the voters should know about your candidate or position.

4. Talent. This is a person who speaks clearly and slowly but with expression. He or she should memorize the message. If you are making a video message, the talent must look directly into the camera lens, appear comfortable, and wear an appropriate expression.

**Helpful hints:**

- Make one or more copies of your finished product. This will be insurance against loss or damage.

- For a steady picture, mount your camera on a tripod.

- Have your talent dress in conservative clothing with solid, muted colors. Do not let sloppy, overly bright, or "busy" clothes detract from your message.

60

# Campaign Staff

See page 53 for suggested use.

Candidate: _____

Campaign manager: _____

Treasurer: _____

Press secretary: _____

Speech writers: _____

_____

Pollsters: _____

_____

Data processors: _____

_____

Campaign workers: _____

_____

_____

# OFFICIAL SYMBOL

_____
(Party Name)

See page 53 for suggested use.

62

# Voter Registration Card

Name: _____
         Last        First

Party: _____

Room #: _____

Grade: _____

*I certify that the information given above is correct.*

Date: _____

Signature: _____

# Voter Registration Card

Name: _____
         Last        First

Party: _____

Room #: _____

Grade: _____

*I certify that the information given above is correct.*

Date: _____

Signature: _____

# Voter Registration Card

Name: _____
         Last        First

Party: _____

Room #: _____

Grade: _____

*I certify that the information given above is correct.*

Date: _____

Signature: _____

# Voter Registration Card

Name: _____
         Last        First

Party: _____

Room #: _____

Grade: _____

*I certify that the information given above is correct.*

Date: _____

Signature: _____

# Election Survey

If the election was held today, would you vote for this candidate?

**Candidate:**

| | Yes | No | Don't Know |
|---|---|---|---|
| 1. _____ | | | |
| 2. _____ | | | |
| 3. _____ | | | |
| 4. _____ | | | |

How do you feel about the following issues?

**Issue:**

| | Support | Oppose | Don't Know |
|---|---|---|---|
| 1. _____ | | | |
| 2. _____ | | | |
| 3. _____ | | | |
| 4. _____ | | | |

How do you think _____ feels about these issues?
(your candidate's name)

| | Supports | Opposes | Don't Know |
|---|---|---|---|
| 1. _____ | | | |
| 2. _____ | | | |
| 3. _____ | | | |
| 4. _____ | | | |

# Campaign Money

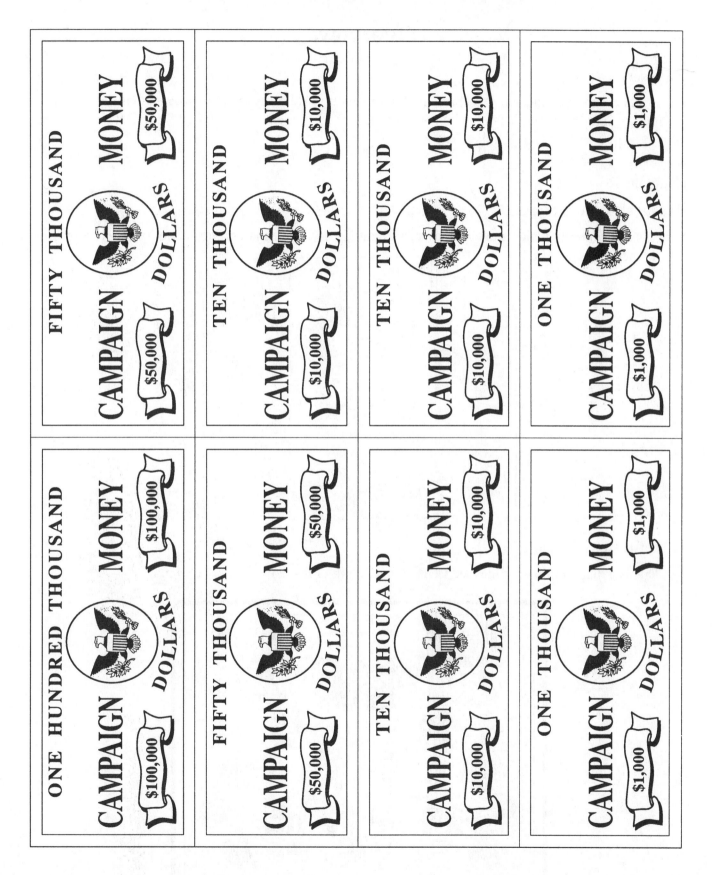

# Electing the President

## Overview

**Purpose:**

The teacher resources and activities presented in this section are designed to expose students to the vocabulary and process associated with the election of the President of the United States. It may also be used to inspire and showcase student work.

**Components:**

### Research Center: (pages 67-78)

- This is a center in which students may work individually or in small groups to complete election unit activities.

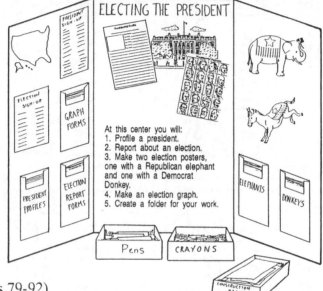

### Bulletin Board: (pages 79-92)

- This is a diagram that outlines the steps to electing the President.

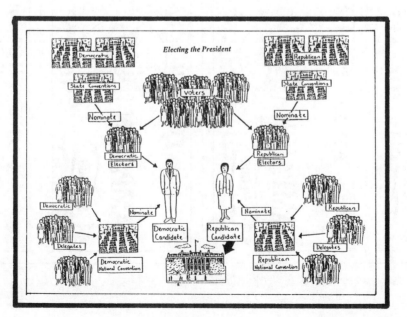

# Research Center of Presidents and Presidential Elections

**Preparation:**

1. Construct your center according to the Research Center Layout diagram (page 68).

2. Collect as many reference materials that contain election information as you can. Almanacs are particularly good sources of statistical information. Do not forget biographies and general historical works for appropriate periods. See the Bibliography (page 93) for a partial listing of appropriate titles.

3. Reproduce, color, and laminate the Presidential Portraits sheets (pages 70-71) and the White House graphic (page 85) and then attach it to the middle section of the center. Also reproduce and attach the President Sign-Up, Election Sign-Up, Electoral Votes map, Republican Elephant, and Democratic Donkey.

4. Trim and attach envelopes.

**Procedure:**

1. Introduce the center to the class.

2. Explain each area of the center.

## President Sign-Up

Groups or individuals select a President about whom they would like to research and report (page 74). Write the name of the group or individual on the line after the President's name. Provide students with cut-outs of presidential portraits to attach to their President Profile sheet (page 75). Groups or individuals are to complete their profiles with the requested information and a brief description of the individual's life and/or accomplishments.

## Election Sign-Up

Groups or individuals select a presidential election that does not include the President they are researching. Mark the Election Sign-Up sheet in the same way as the President Sign-Up sheet. Provide the students with Election Report forms (page 77). Students provide the requested basic facts and add information about the people, issues, events, and outcome of their elections. On the flag they should add the appropriate colors and number of stars for the election year.

## Election Poster

Have students make election posters that are appropriate to their research/report topics. Have them attach the elephant (page 72) or donkey (page 73) symbols to their posters to identify the candidates' parties.

## Election Graph

Using the Election Graph forms (page 78), students plot numbers appropriate to the election studied. For example, they can make a bar graph that compares the popular vote in each state.

# Research Center Layout

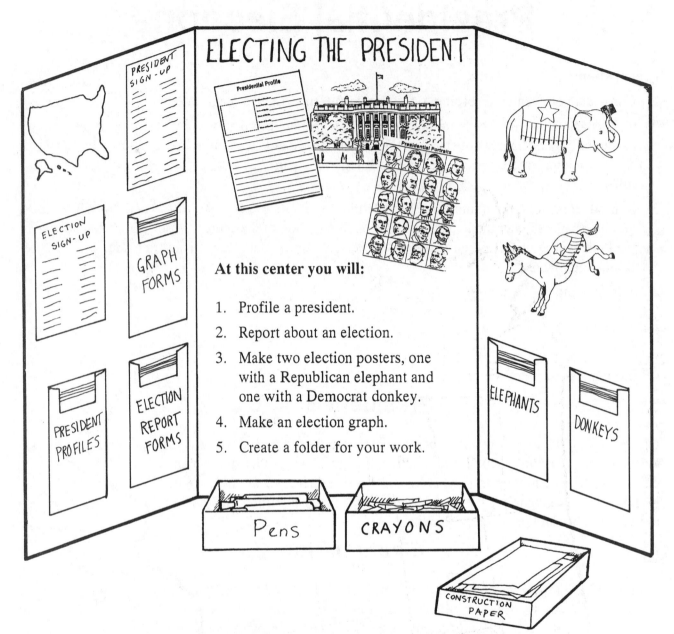

ELECTING THE PRESIDENT

**At this center you will:**

1. Profile a president.
2. Report about an election.
3. Make two election posters, one with a Republican elephant and one with a Democrat donkey.
4. Make an election graph.
5. Create a folder for your work.

## To make this center you will need:

3 sheets of poster board

five 9"x 12" manila mailing envelopes

reference materials

crayons or markers

construction paper

Republican Elephant pattern (page 72, one per student)

Democratic Donkey pattern (page 73, one per student)

President Portraits (pages 70-71)

1 White House graphic (page 85)

1 Electoral Votes Map (page 69)

1 Presidential Sign-Up sheet (page 74)

1 Election Sign-Up sheet (page 76)

Presidential Profile sheets (page 75)

Election Report forms (page 77)

Election Graph forms (page 78)

# Electoral Votes

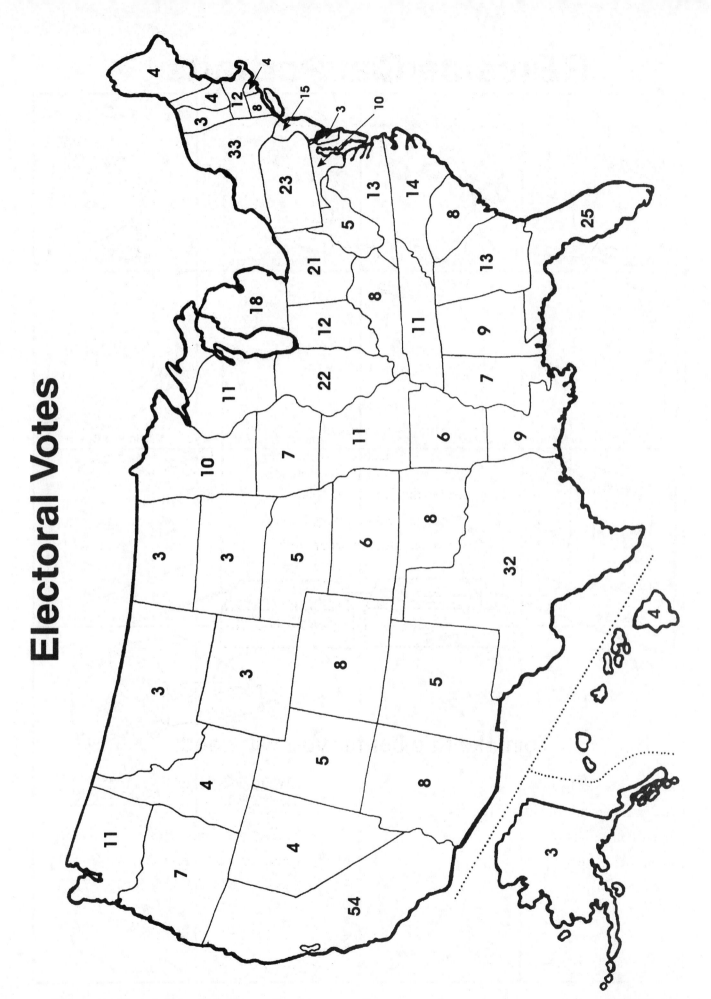

# Presidential Portraits

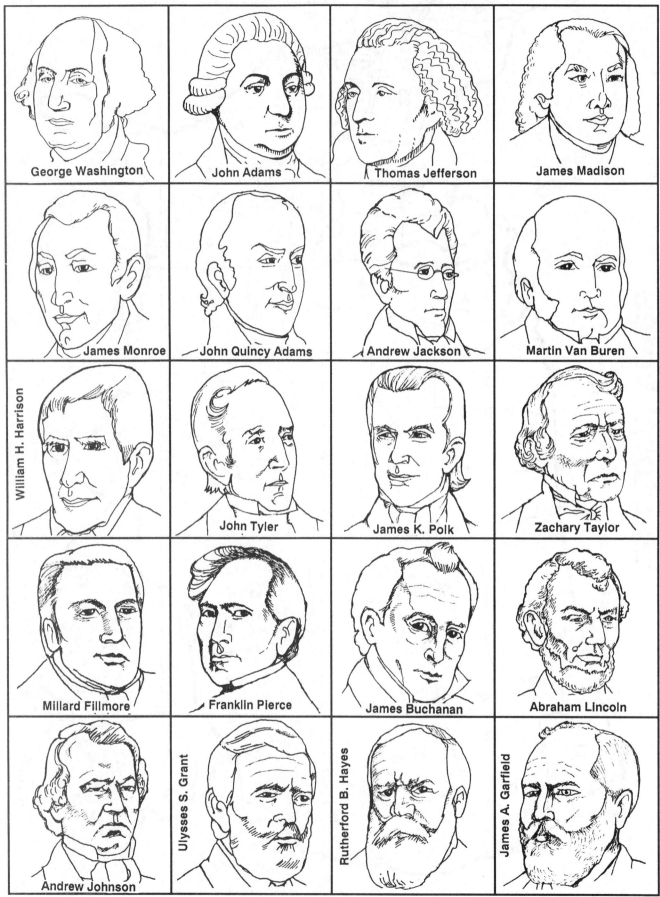

George Washington

John Adams

Thomas Jefferson

James Madison

James Monroe

John Quincy Adams

Andrew Jackson

Martin Van Buren

William H. Harrison

John Tyler

James K. Polk

Zachary Taylor

Millard Fillmore

Franklin Pierce

James Buchanan

Abraham Lincoln

Andrew Johnson

Ulysses S. Grant

Rutherford B. Hayes

James A. Garfield

# Presidential Portraits

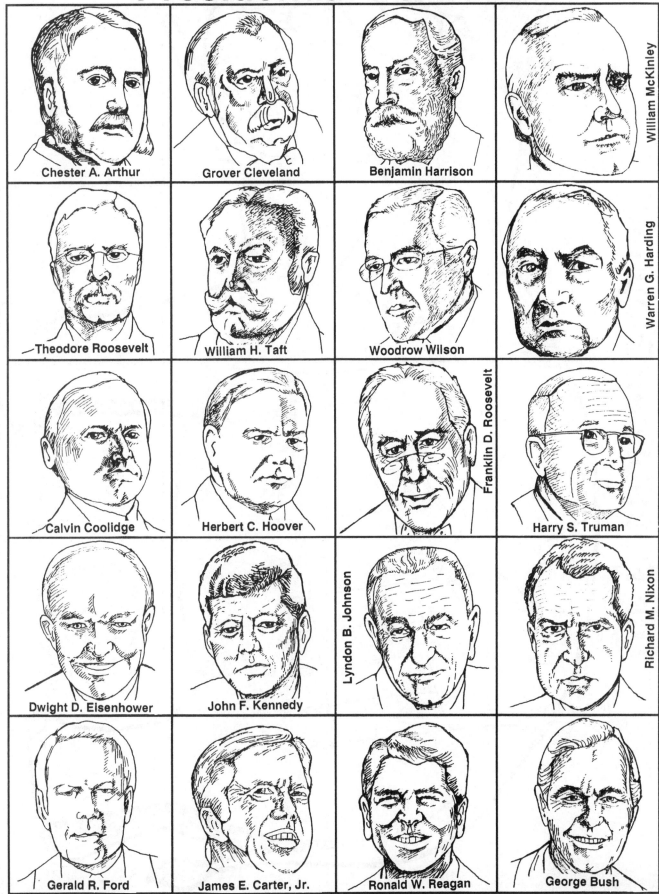

Chester A. Arthur

Grover Cleveland

Benjamin Harrison

William McKinley

Theodore Roosevelt

William H. Taft

Woodrow Wilson

Warren G. Harding

Calvin Coolidge

Herbert C. Hoover

Franklin D. Roosevelt

Harry S. Truman

Dwight D. Eisenhower

John F. Kennedy

Lyndon B. Johnson

Richard M. Nixon

Gerald R. Ford

James E. Carter, Jr.

Ronald W. Reagan

George Bush

# The Republican Elephant

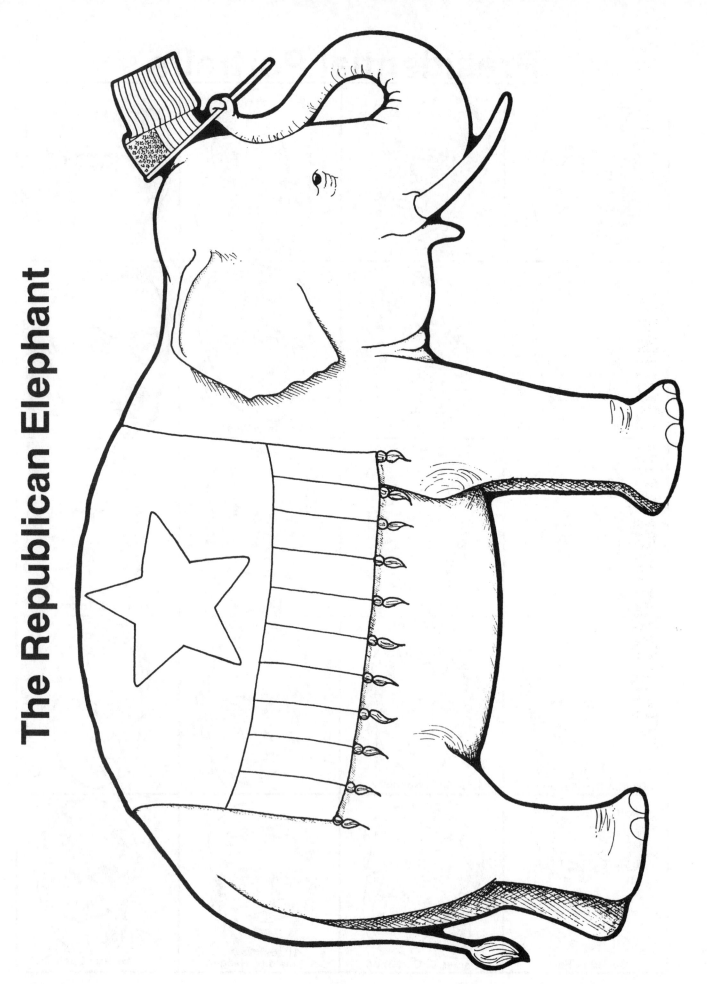

72

# The Democratic Donkey

# Presidential Sign-Up

George Washington _____

John Adams _____

Thomas Jefferson _____

James Madison _____

James Monroe _____

John Quincy Adams _____

Andrew Jackson _____

Martin Van Buren _____

William H. Harrison _____

JohnTyler _____

James Polk _____

Zachary Taylor _____

Millard Fillmore _____

Franklin Pierce _____

James Buchanan _____

Abraham Lincoln _____

Andrew Johnson _____

Ulysses S. Grant _____

Rutherford B. Hayes _____

James A. Garfield _____

Chester A. Arthur _____

Grover Cleveland _____

Benjamin Harrison _____

William McKinley _____

Theodore Roosevelt _____

William H. Taft _____

Woodrow Wilson _____

Warren Harding _____

Calvin Coolidge _____

Herbert Hoover _____

Franklin Roosevelt _____

Harry Truman _____

Dwight Eisenhower _____

John Kennedy _____

Lyndon Johnson _____

Richard Nixon _____

Gerald R. Ford _____

Jimmy Carter _____

Ronald Reagan _____

George Bush _____

# Presidential Profile

_____
(President's Name)

President Number: _____

Years Served: _____

Date of Birth: _____

Place of Birth: _____

Date of Death: _____

Place of Death: _____

_____

_____

_____

_____

_____

_____

_____

_____

_____

_____

_____

# Election Sign-Up

1789: Washington - Adams _____

1792: Washington - Adams _____

1796: Adams - Jefferson _____

1800: Jefferson - Burr _____

1804: Jefferson - Pinckney _____

1808: Madison - Pinckney _____

1812: Madison - Clinton _____

1816: Monroe - King _____

1820: Monroe - none _____

1824: Adams - Jackson _____

1828: Jackson - Adams _____

1832: Jackson - Clay _____

1836: Van Buren - Harrison _____

1840: Harrison- Van Buren _____

1844: Polk - Clay _____

1848: Taylor - Cass _____

1852: Pierce - Scott _____

1856: Buchanan - Fremont _____

1860: Lincoln - Douglas _____

1864: Lincoln - McClellan _____

1868: Grant - Seymour _____

1872: Grant - Greeley _____

1876: Hayes - Tilden _____

1880: Garfield - Hancock _____

1884: Cleveland - Blaine _____

1888: Harrison - Cleveland _____

1892: Cleveland - Harrison _____

1896: McKinley - Bryan _____

1900: McKInley - Bryan _____

1904: Roosevelt - Parker _____

1908: Taft - Bryan _____

1912: Wilson - Roosevelt _____

1916: Wilson - Hughes _____

1920: Harding - Cox _____

1924: Coolidge - Davis _____

1928: Hoover - Smith _____

1932: Roosevelt - Hoover _____

1936: Roosevelt - Landon _____

1940: Roosevelt - Wilkie _____

1944: Roosevelt - Dewey _____

1948: Truman - Dewey _____

1952: Eisenhower - Stevenson _____

1956: Eisenhower - Stevenson _____

1960: Kennedy - Nixon _____

1964: Johnson - Goldwater _____

1968: Nixon - Humphrey _____

1972: Nixon - McGovern _____

1976: Carter - Ford _____

1980: Reagan - Carter _____

1984: Reagan - Mondale _____

1988: Bush - Dukakis _____

1992: _____

# Election Report

The Year: _____

The Candidates:

_____

_____

_____

_____

_____

_____

_____

_____

_____

_____

_____

_____

_____

_____

_____

_____

_____

_____

# Election Graph
## For the year: _____

# Bulletin Board Diagram of the Electoral Process

**Preparation:**

1. Select an area in the room where you or the students can assemble the bulletin board as the unit progresses.

2. Construct the bulletin board according to the Bulletin Board Diagram on page 80.

**Helpful Hints:**

Use the originals or make copies of the diagram components on pages 81 through 91 and mount them after they have been laminated.

Have students write reports or definitions that describe the steps to electing the President. Mount them next to the appropriate parts of the diagram.

Add arrows and labels as terms are introduced or the corresponding events occur. (The diagram illustrated on page 80 traces the 1988 election.)

Post clippings of newspaper or magazine articles and pictures next to the appropriate sections of the diagram.

Have students create labels to add to the diagram that identify specific people, locations, dates, and numbers.

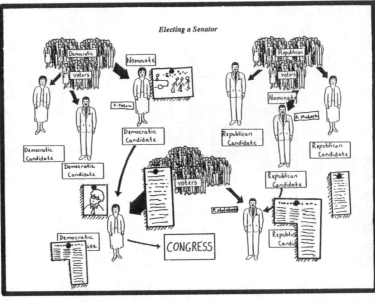

**Note:**

Although the components were designed for the suggested bulletin board described above, it is possible to use them to design a diagram that traces the steps of a non-presidential election. One suggested layout is illustrated on page 92.

## Bulletin Board Diagram
*Electing the President*

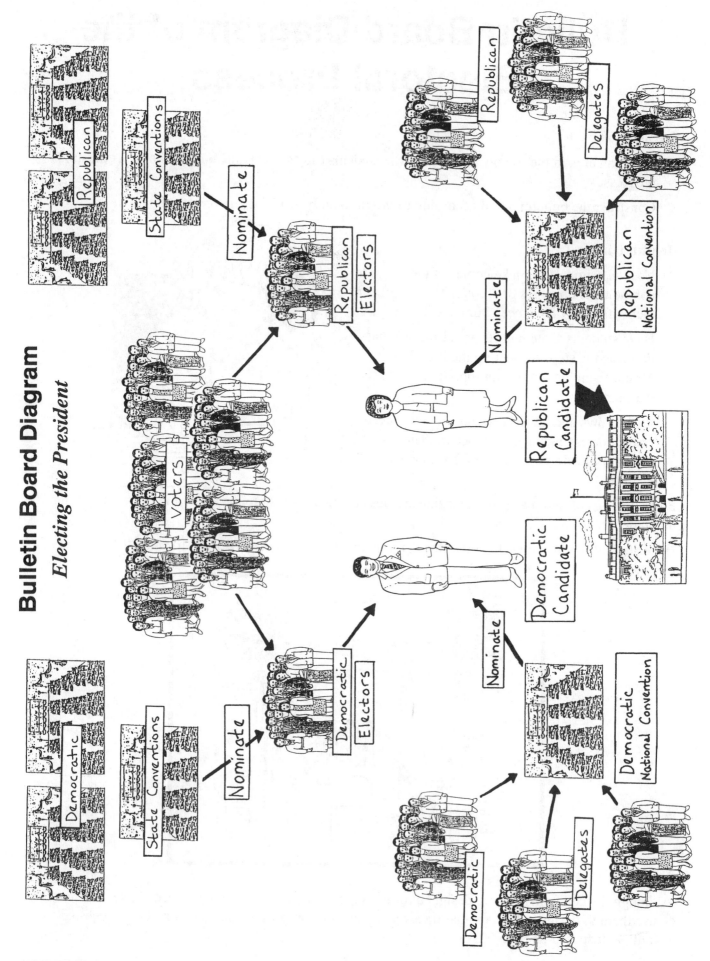

# Candidate

# Candidate

# Electors

# Convention Floor

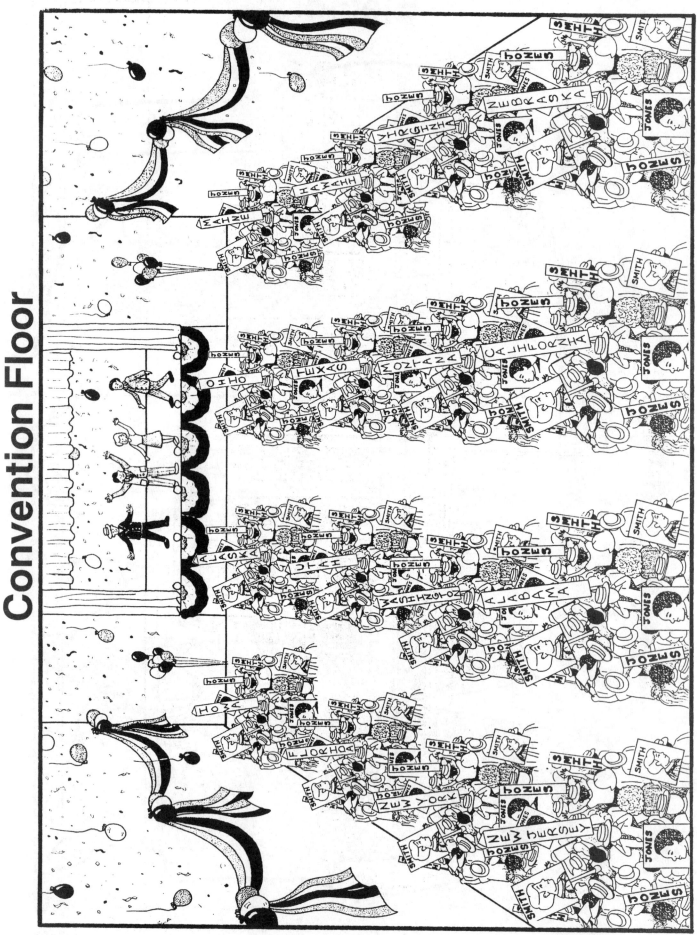

84

# The White House

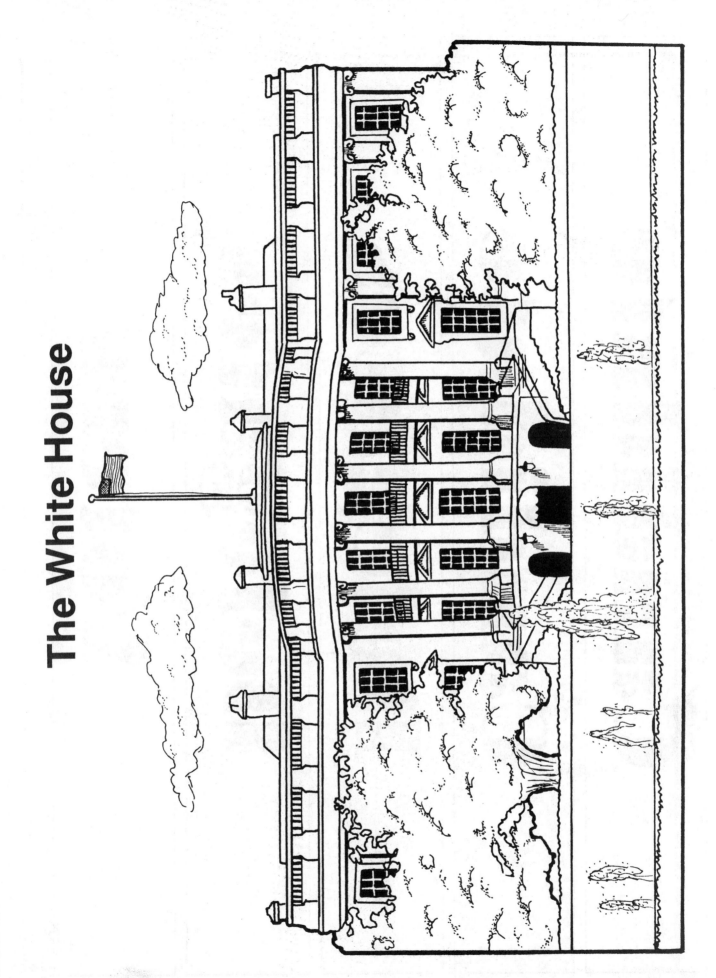

Candidate

Candidate

Delegates

Delegates

Voters

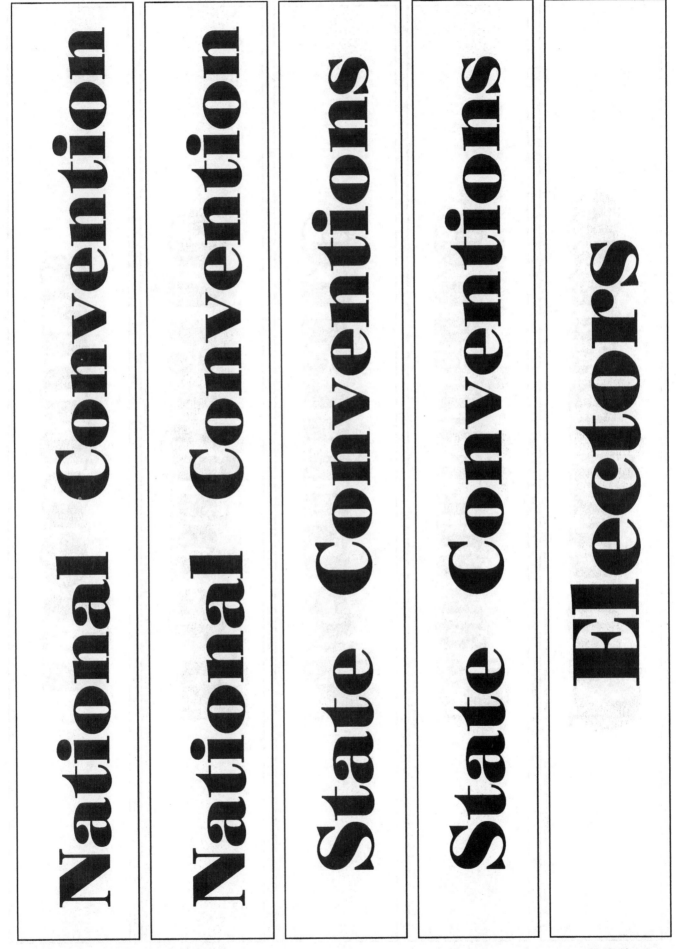

National Convention

National Convention

State Conventions

State Conventions

Electors

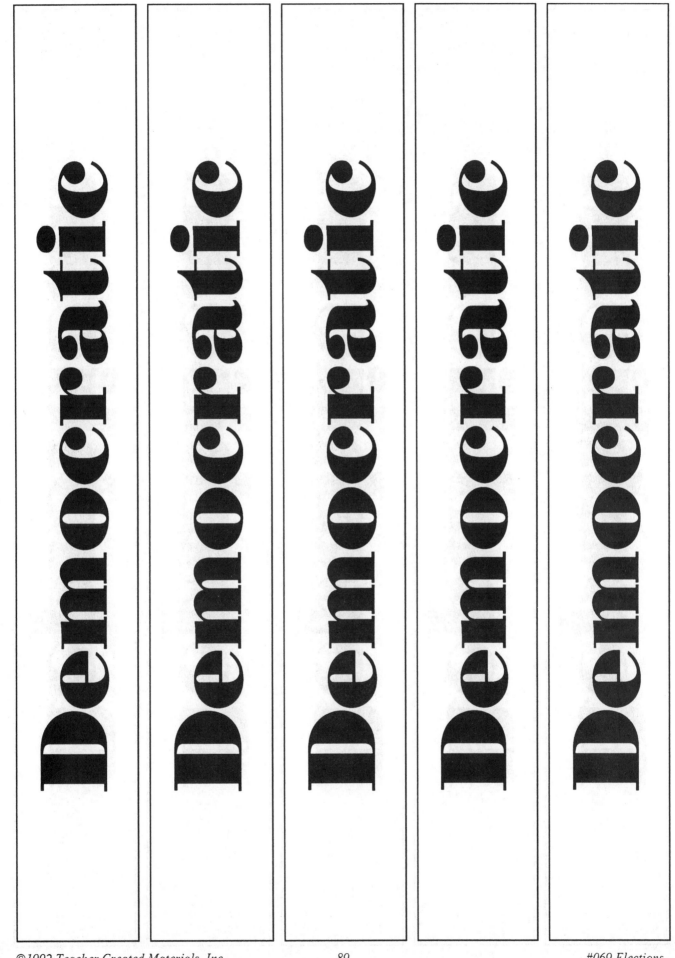

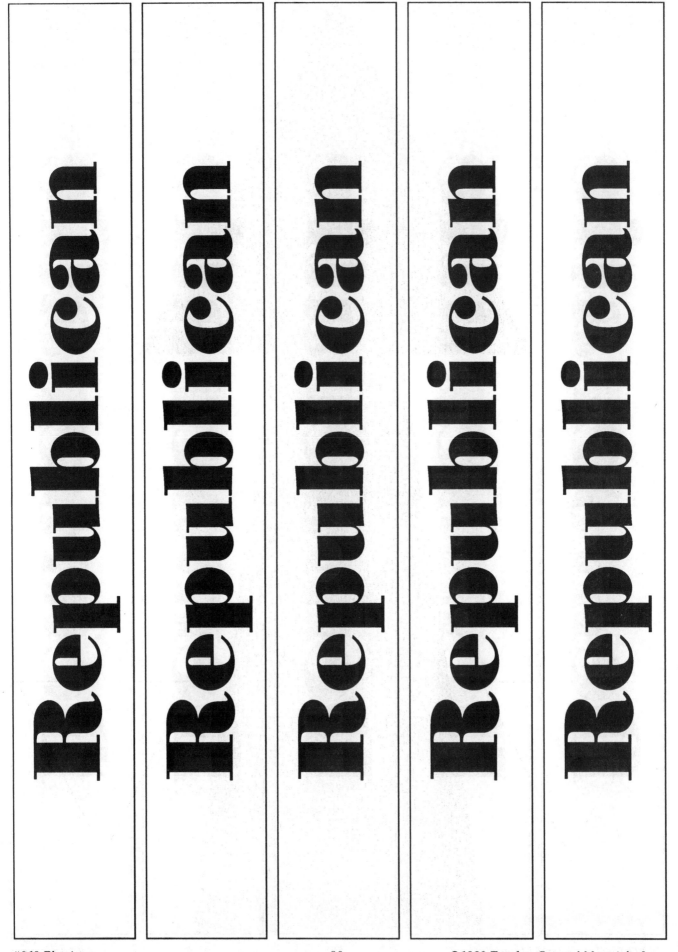

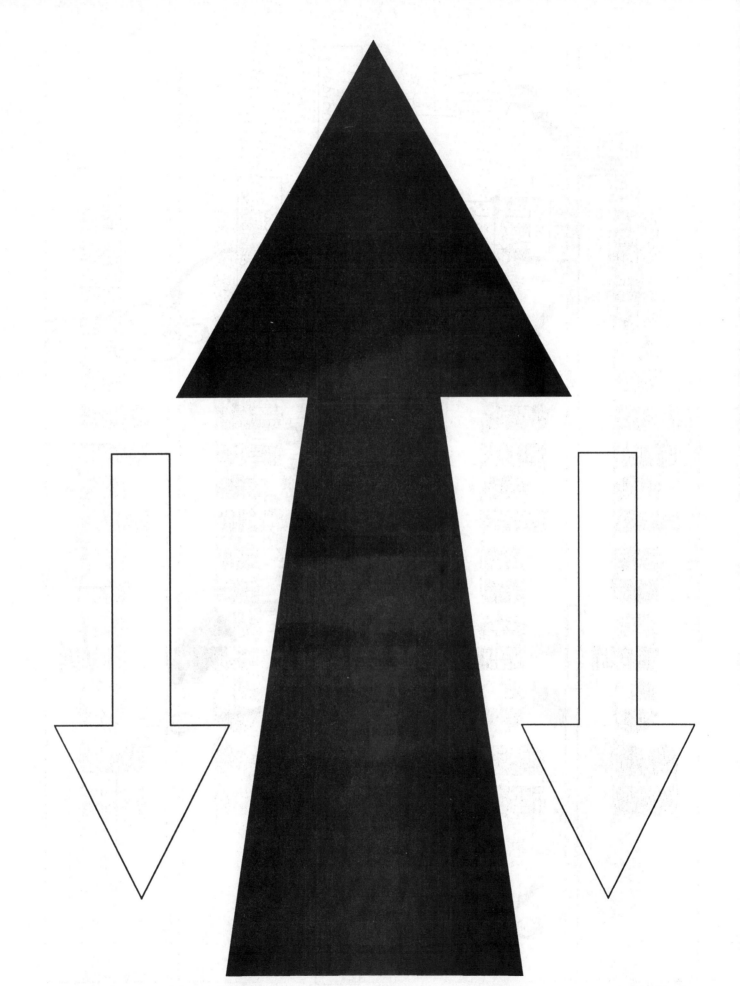

## Bulletin Board Diagram
### Electing a Senator

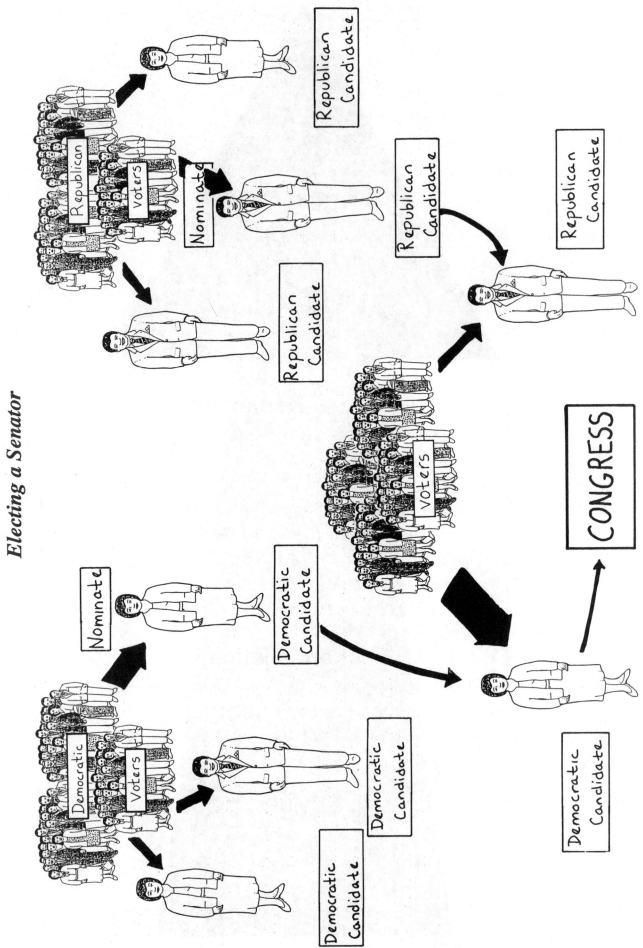

Republican Candidate

Republican Candidate

Republican Candidate

Republican Candidate

Republican Voters

Nominate

CONGRESS

Voters

Democratic Candidate

Democratic Candidate

Democratic Candidate

Democratic Candidate

Democratic Voters

Nominate

92

# Bibliography
## The Constitution

Aten, Jerry. *Our Living Constitution, Then and Now.* (Good Apple, Inc. 1987)

Colman, Warren. *The Constitution.* (Children's Press, 1987)

Fritz, Jean. *Shh! We're Writing the Constitution.* (G.P. Putnam's Sons, 1987)

Hauptly, Denis J. *A Convention of Delegates: The Creation of the Constitution.* (Atheneum, 1987)

Katz, William Loren, and Gaughran, Bernard. *The Constitutional Amendments.* (Franklin Watts, Inc., 1974)

Lindrop, Edmund. *Birth of the Constitution.* (Enslow Publishers, Inc., 1987)

Maestro, Betsy, and Maestro, Giulio. *A More Perfect Union: The Story of Our Constitution.* (Lothrop, Lee, and Shepard, 1987)

Peterson, Helen Stone. *The Making of the Constitution.* (Garrard Publishing Co., 1974)

Stein, R. Conrad. *The Story of the Ninteenth Amendment.* (Children's Press, 1982)

Witty, Paul, and Kohler, Julilly. *You and the Constitution of the United States.* (Children's Press, 1948).

## Elections-Nonfiction

Fradin, Dennis B. *Voting and Elections.* (Children's Press, 1985)

Gray, Lee Learner. *How We Choose a President.* (St. Martin's Press, 1976)

Hargrove, Jim. *The Story of Presidential Elections.* (Children's Press, 1988)

Lindop, Edmund. *The First Book of Elections.* (Franklin Watts, 1968)

Peterson, Helen Stone. *Electing Our Presidents.* (Garrard Publishing Co., 1970)

Phelen, Mary Kay. *Election Day.* (Thomas Y. Crowell Company, 1967)

Weingast, David E. *We Elect a President.* (Julian Messner, 1968)

Wise, William. *Leader's, Laws, and Citizens: The Story of Democracy and Government.* (Parent's Magazine Press, 1973)

## Elections-Fiction

Cohen, Dan. *The Mystery of the Hidden Camera.* (Carolrhoda Books, 1979)

Hermes, Patricia. *Heads, I Win.* (Harcourt Brace Jovanovich, 1988)

Hughes, Dean. *Nutty for President.* (Bantam, 1986)

Hurwitz, Johanna. *Class President.* (Morrow Junior Books, 1990)

Littke, Lael. *Trish for President.* (Harcourt Brace Jovanovich, 1984)

Morris, Judy K. *The Kid Who Ran for Principal.* (Lippincott, 1989)

Morton, Jane. *I Am Rubber, You Are Glue.* (Beaufort Books, 1981)

Park, Barbara. *Rosie Swanson: Fourth Grade Geek for President.* (A.A. Knopf, 1991)

Perl, Lila. *Don't Ask Miranda.* (Seabury Press, 1979)

Singer, Marilyn. *The Case of the Fixed Election.* (Harper and Row, 1989)

# Answer Key

## page 14

| | | |
|---|---|---|
| 1. f | 6. d | 11. b |
| 2. c | 7. a | 12. g |
| 3. j | 8. e | 13. a |
| 4. h | 9. a | 14. a |
| 5. a | 10. i | 15. b |

## page 15

1. no; Mr. A is 22 years old. To be a representative a citizen must be 25 years old; Article I, Section 2.2.
2. no; Miss B has been a citizen of the United States for six years. To be a senator a person must have been a citizen for nine years; Article I, Section 3.3.
3. no; Even though Mrs. C is a citizen, she has been living in the United States for only four years. To be eligible to run for President, a citizen must have been living in the country for 14 years; Article 2, Section 1.5.
4. no; Each state is allowed two senators no matter what size it is; Article I, Section 3.1.
5. yes; Representation in Congress is determined by population. If the population of a state decreases, the number of representatives from that state may be reduced; Article 1, Section 2.3.

## page 16

1. no; The 15th Amendment prohibits denying citizens the right to vote because of their race.
2. yes; The 19th Amendment guarantees the right of citizens to vote whether they are men or women.
3. no; The 22nd Amendment prohibits anyone from holding more than two terms as president.
4. yes; The 17th Amendment gives citizens the right to elect their senators directly.
5. yes; The 26th Amendment gives citizens the right to vote when they reach the age of eighteen years.
6. no; The 24th Amendment prohibits governments from charging a tax to vote.
7. no; The 23rd Amendment gives the District of Columbia three electoral votes.

## page 17

1. direct election - the people themselves choose their public officials
2. indirect election - people elect representatives who will choose public officials on their behalf
3. nonpartisan election - parties of the candidates are not identified
4. runoff - If no candidate in certain elections wins a majority of the votes cast, this election is held to choose between the two candidates who polled the highest number of votes

5. special election - held to fill an office that has become vacant before the end of a term
6. primary election - held to choose from among candidates of a party the person who will represent the party in a general election
7. closed primary election - voters must pick their political party before entering the voting booth and who then choose from among candidates on their party's ballot only.
8. open primary election - voters receive ballots for all parties, but vote on ballots of only one party once they are in the voting booth
9. blanket primary election - voters choose candidates from all parties
10. indirect election.
11. Answers will vary.

## page 18

Federal election days are November 3, November 8, November 2, and November 7

## page 19

1. Australian ballot - presented to a voter at a polling place and marked in secret
2. party column ballot - candidates are listed by party
3. office-block ballot - candidates are listed by office
4. short ballot - candidates for only a small number of offices are listed
5. Australian ballot
6. Bonus: Ballot comes from Ballotte (French) which means little ball. This refers to the practice in ancient Athens of casting votes using stones or balls of different types which stood for different choices.

## page 21

1. election 2. vote 3. ballots 4. candidate 5. incumbents 6. campaign 7. Democratic 8. Republican 9. general 10. electors 11. electoral 12. delegate 13. primary

## page 22

| | | | |
|---|---|---|---|
| 1. voter | | 6. | candidate |
| 2. Democratic, Republican | | 7. | campaign |
| 3. election day | | 8. | electoral |
| 4. ballot | | 9. | absentee |
| 5. delegates | | 10. | incumbent |

## pages 23, 24, 25

Answers and location will vary depending on locale and year.

# Answer Key *(cont.)*

## page 26

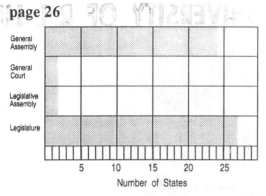

5. 100

6, 7. Answers will vary.

## page 27

| Age | Citizenship |
|-----|-------------|
| 25 years old | 7 years of citizenship |
| **Residence** | **Term** |
| inhabitant of his/her state | elected every 2 years |

1, 2, 3, 4. Answers vary with locale.

## page 28

500,000

How areas are outlined varies, but areas enclosed must contain 500,000 people.

## page 29

| Age | Citizenship |
|-----|-------------|
| 30 years old | 9 years of citizenship |
| **Residence** | **Term** |
| inhabitant of his/her state | serves 6 years |

1. 2  2. 100, 3. 33  4. entire state  5. A. 1998  B. 2000, 2002

## page 31

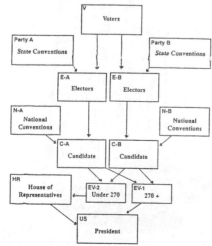

## page 32

A. Electoral Votes

41-50

31-40

21-30

11-20

3-10

B. red: CA

blue: NY. TX

green: IL, OH, PA

yellow: WA, WI, TN, GA, N.C., VA, MA, NJ

uncolored: all others

## page 33

1.   4,784,000

2.   4,536,000

3.   States 2, 3, 4; 40 electoral votes

4.   States 1, 5; 50 electoral votes

5.   Candidate B won the election because he received the most electoral votes.

## page 34

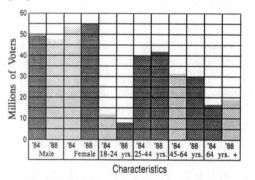

6. yes, 7. yes, 8. no, 9. yes, 10. no

## page 35

| | | | | | |
|---|---|---|---|---|---|
| 1. P | 9. M | 17. P | 25. M | 33. M | 41. M |
| 2. M | 10. P | 18. P | 26. M | 34. M | 42. M |
| 3. M | 11. M | 19. M | 27. M | 35. P | |
| 4. M | 12. M | 20. M | 28. M | 36. M | |
| 5. P | 13. M | 21. M | 29. M | 37. P | |
| 6. M | 14. P | 22. M | 30. M | 38. M | |
| 7. P | 15. P | 23. P | 31. M | 39. M | |
| 8. M | 16. P | 24. P | 32. P | 40. M | |

Largest majority—Lyndon Johnson

Smallest plurality—John Quincy Adams

# Answer Key *(cont.)*

**page 36**

1. Abraham Lincoln, Ulysses S. Grant, Rutherford B. Hayes, James A. Garfield, Benjamin Harrison, William McKinley , Theodore Roosevelt, William Howard Taft, Warren G. Harding, Calvin Coolidge, Herbert Hoover, Dwight D. Eisenhower, Richard M. Nixon, Ronald W. Reagan, George H.W. Bush

2. Andrew Johnson, Chester A. Arthur, Theodore Roosevelt, Calvin Coolidge, Richard M. Nixon, George H.W. Bush

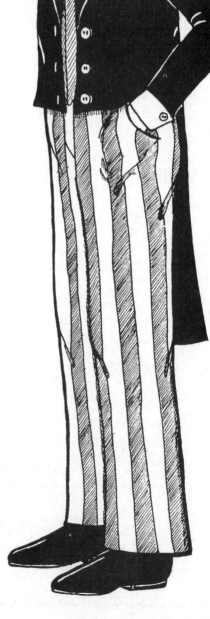

3. 1864, 1868, 1872, 1876, 1880, 1884, 1888, 1892, 1896, 1900, 1904, 1908, 1912, 1916, 1920, 1924, 1928, 1932, 1936, 1940, 1944, 1948, 1952, 1956, 1960, 1964, 1968, 1972, 1976, 1980, 1984, 1988

**page 37**

1. Andrew Jackson, Martin Van Buren, James K. Polk, Franklin Pierce, James Buchanan, Grover Cleveland , Woodrow Wilson, Franklin D. Roosevelt, Harry S. Truman, John F. Kennedy, Lyndon B. Johnson, James E. Carter

2. Martin Van Buren, Franklin D. Roosevelt, Harry S. Truman, Lyndon B. Johnson

3. 1836, 1840, 1844, 1852, 1856, 1860, 1864, 1868, 1872, 1876, 1880, 1884, 1888, 1892, 1896, 1900, 1904, 1908, 1912, 1916, 1920, 1924, 1928, 1932, 1936, 1940, 1944, 1948, 1952, 1956, 1960, 1964, 1968, 1972, 1976, 1980, 1984, 1988

**page 38**

1. Federalist  2. Federalist   3. Democratic-Republican
4. Democratic-Republican 5. Democratic-Republican
6. Whig 7. Whig 8. Whig  9. Whig

**page 39**

1. Anti-Masonic, Andrew Jackson, 2. Free Soil, Zachary Taylor, 3. American Know Nothing, James Buchanan, 4. Democratic Secessionist, Abraham Lincoln, 5. Populist, Grover Cleveland, 6. "Bull Moose" Progressive, Woodrow Wilson, 7. Socialist, Woodrow Wilson, 8. Progressive, Calvin Coolidge, 9. States' Rights Dixiecrats, Harry Truman, 10.  American Independent, Richard Nixon, 11. National Unity, Ronald Reagan